INTRODUCING
THE GREAT
AMERICAN NOVEL

INTRODUCING THE GREAT AMERICAN NOVEL

Edited by Anne Skillion

*A New York Public Library
Publishing Project*

A STONESONG PRESS BOOK
Quill · William Morrow · New York

Copyright © 1988 by The Stonesong Press
Acknowledgments, constituting a continuation of the copyright page,
are listed on pages 255–256.

Library of Congress Cataloging-in-Publication Data

Introducing the great American novel / edited by Anne Skillion.
   p.   cm.
  "A Stonesong Press book."
  "A New York Public Library publishing project."
  ISBN 0-688-07346-8
  ISBN 0-688-08065-0 (pbk.)
  1. American fiction—History and criticism. 2. American Prose
literature. I. Skillion, Anne. II. New York (City). Public
Library.
PS371.I5   1988
813'.009—dc19   87-38319
                                             CIP

Printed in the United States of America

First Quill Edition

1 2 3 4 5 6 7 8 9 10

BOOK DESIGN BY DALE COTTON

Preface

Introductions and commentaries serve many purposes: They invite and bring the reader to the work, often providing a framework for understanding the novels in their deepest dimensions; they introduce the reader to the life and times of the author, sometimes giving perspective to biographical elements in the otherwise fictional work, elucidating little-known facts about the author, and giving insight into the creative process itself. What a loss to anyone who has ever read Faulkner's *Sanctuary* if he missed the author's own fascinating introduction in which he frankly admitted among other things that the book was "a cheap idea . . . deliberately conceived to make money." Or, when one knows that H. L. Mencken was a close friend of Theodore Dreiser, one comes closer to the spirit behind *An American Tragedy:* "He would sit down at his desk, in the days when I saw him oftenest, and bang away with pen and ink for four or five hours. The stuff poured out of him almost automatically. . . ."

As I reviewed the essays collected in this volume, I was struck by a recurring theme that runs through them—from Hawthorne to Dreiser to Richard Wright to Kurt Vonnegut: the constant necessity of maintaining an intrepid spirit in the face of adversity. That ethos of perseverance along with a synthesis of voices from many heritages is a characteristic shared by The New York Public

5

Library. It permeates our institution even today. Like great American literature, we hope to enlighten, entertain, and preserve.

The resources of the research collections of The New York Public Library now number over thirty million cataloged items. These have come to us from generous collectors and benefactors over the years, and we add to them constantly. But our responsibility is not only to acquire, organize, and preserve. I see our vocation as larger and more dynamic. We must reach out into the community. This book, and others with which we are involved through support or active research, is a source of special satisfaction for me because it is a sharing of our resources and the skills of a research librarian. *Introducing the Great American Novel* has been derived from material we conserve, and it goes beyond the confines of our building and city to all those who love the printed word.

Bringing these essays together in one thematic source is a role we play with relish, for many are obscure, long out of print, or not very well known. When the New York Public Library can publicize fine writing and thereby stimulate more reading, we are doubly satisfied.

—VARTAN GREGORIAN
The New York Public Library
1987

Contents

Contents

Contents

Introduction

Some years ago—I still cringe to think of the brass in doing such a thing—I wrote Ernest Hemingway and asked him if he would write an introduction to a slim volume I had written about pitching as a participatory journalist in an All-Star baseball game in Yankee Stadium. I sent the proofs of the book to him in Ketchum, Idaho, and said the "Introduction" didn't need to be lengthy—just a couple of pages. I'm not even sure I sent a stamped and self-addressed envelope in which to include what I was sure he was bound to produce.

Hemingway resisted the opportunity. But he did send me a short but pleasant blurb, including the felicitous phrase that in the book (*Out of My League*) I had described the "dark side of the moon of Walter Mitty"—which the publisher instantly slapped on the book's jacket along with Hemingway's name in letters almost as large as my own. I didn't mind a bit.

Last summer I was describing this to John Knowles, who told me that he felt the success of his classic A *Separate Peace* was due in large part to such a blurb. Apparently in this country the book had been turned down by every publishing house of note. Finally it was accepted by Secker and Warburg in England. On its publication, E. M. Forster read a copy, and he was so impressed that he wrote Knowles a letter comparing the book to the *Philoctetes* of Sophocles in its treatment of physical prowess, pain, and betrayal.

11

On the strength of this remarkable encomium Macmillan (Knowles's American publisher) felt comfortable about publishing the book. Their editors knew that the reviewers would have to treat the book seriously. Which indeed they did.

What we have in this present volume are in essence blurbs *in extenso*—reflective essays, mostly introductions, by distinguished authors on their fellow writers' work, often evaluations that by their interpretive acumen have served in some cases to resurrect and promote the work itself.

Contemporary literature has many such examples. Allan Bloom's rather dense tome, *The Closing of the American Mind*—the thrust suggesting that students are not only unaware of the basic history of our civilization but what's more don't care—got an enormous boost from Saul Bellow. He persuaded Bloom to expand an article called "Our Listless Universities" (published in *The National Review*) into a book and provided an introduction for it. What he wrote—as in the case of Forster and *A Separate Peace*—commanded the attention of the top critics and helped *The Closing of the American Mind* to climb to the top of *The New York Times* best-seller list.

An even more striking example of the impact of an important introduction would surely be Malcolm Cowley's foreword to William Faulkner's work in the Viking "Portable" series. Faulkner's literary fortunes had sunk to such a level that after the war only one book, *Sanctuary*, was in print; the publishers had melted down the copper plates of the other novels to donate to the war effort. It was only with much persuasion on the part of Cowley that Viking decided to include Faulkner in its series. In his introduction Cowely got Faulkner to help him with an outline of the Yoknapatawpha County saga. Indeed, when the Portable was published to considerable acclaim, renewing interest in the author, Cowley got an inscribed copy from Faulkner: "Damn you, you've done what was supposed to be the occupation of my declining years!"

This volume does not include that introduction, though Cowley is represented by his essay on F. Scott Fitzgerald, which introduced *The Great Gatsby* in the Modern Library Edition of Fitzgerald's *Three Novels*—a focus on the novelist's pecuniary obsessions that finds a modern-day echo in the phenomenon of the yuppies and their fascination with the process of making and spending money.

The variety in the selection of these introductions and essays is considerable. There are the literary assessments—among them Saul Bellow on Ralph Ellison's *Invisible Man*, Jean-Paul Sartre on John Dos Passos and *1919*, Lionel Trilling on *The Bostonians*, Alfred Kazin on *Moby-Dick*, Irving Howe on Edith Wharton, and Tom Wolfe on Norman Mailer's *An American Dream*, this last a wonderfully perky account of Mailer taking on Dostoevski with the serial novel ("Son of Crime and Punishment," the article is called) and coming up very much wanting—the only essay in the collection that would tend to make the author under discussion wince a few times.

Sometimes we learn little nubbits of information about the introducer himself: T. S. Eliot, in his introduction to *Huckleberry Finn*, discloses that he never read the Twain novel as a boy, suspecting that his parents kept the book out of his hands for fear he would pick up some of Huck's bad habits, in particular a taste for tobacco.

The most interesting accounts at least to me—are personal accounts: Ford Madox Ford, in his introduction to an edition of *A Farewell to Arms*, describing how Ernest Hemingway took over an issue of the *Transatlantic Review* just as it was about to go to press (the editor, Ford, was on a trip away from Paris) and cut the text of most of the scheduled contributors to just a line or so, substituting in their place—as Ford put it—"his wildest friends" . . . certainly the ultimate nightmare for those like myself who struggle at editing a literary magazine. Or H. L. Mencken's portrait of Theodore Dreiser in his introduction to *An American Tragedy*—emphasizing the author's obsession for detail ("when he described a street in Chicago and New York it was always a street that he knew as intimately as the policeman on the beat"). Or Maxwell Perkins repeating a description he had heard of "the great figure of Thomas Wolfe, advancing in his long countryman's stride, with his swaying black raincoat, and what he was chanting was, 'I wrote ten thousand words today—I wrote ten thousand words today.' "Or William

Faulkner, in his introduction to the Modern Library edition of *Sanctuary*, recounting his invention of the most "horrific tale" he could think of to make money, completing the work in three weeks' time, and then his publisher aghast reaction: "Good God, I can't publish this. We'd both be in jail!"

On occasion an introduction serves to air a grievance . . . as in Tennessee Williams using his forward to Carson McCullers's *Reflections in a Golden Eye* to ruminate about critics—specifically their inclination to condemn second novels if the first has been a great success. Williams feels this can be set down as physical law, and so obsessed is he with this and other complaints that it isn't for quite a stretch that he finally gets around to concentrating on McCullers.

If there is a thread common to these introductions it is to suggest the parlous relationship between the writer and the editor, the critics, and eventually the reading public. The great Scribners editor Maxwell Perkins takes up the editor-writer partnership in his introduction to the Thomas Wolfe collection on its presentation to the Harvard College Library. He recounts his association with Wolfe from their first meeting ("Wolfe was a turbulent spirit and . . . we were in for turbulence") through their editorial travails (on *Of Time and the River* the two worked for a year of "nights of work, including Sundays, and every cut, and change, and interpolation, was argued about and about") and to their eventual parting and the dissolving of literature's most famous editor-writer relationship.

How often the texts indicate the woes and vicissitudes of fiction writing! In his evaluation of Hawthorne's *The Scarlet Letter* Henry James describes an incident in which the author "in a very desponding mood" hurries after his publisher and presses a manuscript into his hand. "It is either very good or very bad." In his introduction to *The Day of the Locust* Budd Schulberg quotes from a letter Nathanael West wrote to F. Scott Fitzgerald following the book's publication: "So far the box score stands: Good reviews—fifteen percent, bad reviews—twenty-five percent, brutal personal attacks—sixty percent." The royalties realized for "contributing this risible and terrifying little masterpiece to our permanent library" (as Schulberg described the novel) only amounted to five hundred dollars.

Publishers as well as critics get their lumps. Theodore Dreiser, according to H. L. Mencken, thought of publishers as a class of people to be grouped with "kidnappers, dope fiends, and pirates on the high seas." A prefatory note to *The Red Badge of Courage* mentions that Stephen Crane did not even get support from his *family*. They thought of his *Maggie: A Girl of the Streets* as a book that was "not nice," as they phrased it, and they burned the copies he sent them. In fact, most of the initial printing of eleven hundred copies was sold for kindling, much of it ending up in Crane's own boardinghouse stove to get him through the winter. Yes indeed! That first printing of Crane's certainly could have used the likes of the introduction that grace this volume.

That surely must be a writer's common daydream as the final paragraph is finished and the cover is put back on the typewriter: Who might be interested in doing an introduction to what I've done. Or at the very least a blurb. It can make all the difference!

—George Plimpton

HENRY JAMES ON

The Scarlet Letter
by Nathaniel Hawthorne, 1850

When the young Henry James was asked to write a study of Hawthorne for the British series English Men of Letters, *he told Hawthorne's son Julian, "I don't want to do it; I'm not competent. And yet if I don't, some Englishman will do it worse than I would." This essay on* The Scarlet Letter *is drawn from his now renowned* Hawthorne *of 1879.*

His publisher, Mr. Fields, in a volume entitled *Yesterdays with Authors,* has related the circumstances in which Hawthorne's masterpiece came into the world. "In the winter of 1849, after he had been ejected from the Customhouse, I went down to Salem to see him and inquire after his health, for we heard he had been suffering from illness. He was then living in a modest wooden house. . . . I found him alone in a chamber over the sitting-room of the dwelling, and as the day was cold he was hovering near a stove. We fell into talk about his future prospects, and he was, as I feared I should find him, in a very desponding mood." His visitor urged him to bethink himself of publishing something, and Hawthorne replied by calling his attention to the small popularity his published productions had yet acquired, and declaring he had done nothing and had no spirit for doing anything. The narrator of the incident urged upon him the necessity of a more hopeful view of his situation, and proceeded to take leave. He had not reached the street, however, when Hawthorne hurried to overtake him, and, placing a roll of MS. in his hand, bade him take it to Boston, read it, and pronounce upon it. "It is either very good or very bad," said the author; "I don't know which." "On my way back to Boston," says Mr. Fields, "I read the germ of *The Scarlet*

Letter; before I slept that night I wrote him a note all aglow with admiration of the marvellous story he had put into my hands, and told him that I would come again to Salem the next day and arrange for its publication. I went on in such an amazing state of excitement, when we met again in the little house, that he would not believe I was really in earnest. He seemed to think I was beside myself, and laughed sadly at my enthusiasm." Hawthorne, however, went on with the book and finished it, but it appeared only a year later. His biographer quotes a passage from a letter which he wrote in February, 1850, to his friend Horatio Bridge. "I finished my book only yesterday; one end being in the press at Boston, while the other was in my head here at Salem, so that, as you see, my story is at least fourteen miles long. . . . My book, the publisher tells me, will not be out before April. He speaks of it in tremendous terms of approbation; so does Mrs. Hawthorne, to whom I read the conclusion last night. It broke her heart, and sent her to bed with a grievous headache—which I look upon as a triumphant success. Judging from the effect upon her and the publisher, I may calculate on what bowlers call a ten-strike. But I don't make any such calculation." And Mr. Lathrop calls attention, in regard to this passage, to an allusion in the *English Note-Books* (September 14, 1855). "Speaking of Thackeray, I cannot but wonder at his coolness in respect to his own pathos, and compare it to my emotions when I read the last scene of *The Scarlet Letter* to my wife, just after writing it—tried to read it rather, for my voice swelled and heaved as if I were tossed up and down on an ocean as it subsides after a storm. But I was in a very nervous state then, having gone through a great diversity of emotion while writing it, for many months."

The work has the tone of the circumstances in which it was produced. If Hawthorne was in a sombre mood, and if his future was painfully vague, *The Scarlet Letter* contains little enough of gaiety or of hopefulness. It is densely dark, with a single spot of vivid colour in it; and it will probably long remain the most consistently gloomy of English novels of the first order. But I just now called it the author's masterpiece, and I imagine it will continue to be, for other generations than ours, his most substantial title to fame. The subject had probably lain a long time in his mind, as his subjects were apt to do; so that he appears completely to possess it, to know it and feel it. It is simpler and more complete than his other novels; it achieves more perfectly what it attempts, and it has about it that charm, very hard to express, which we find in an artist's work the first time he has touched his highest mark—a sort of straightness and naturalness of execution, an unconsciousness of his public, and freshness of interest in his theme. It was a great success, and he immediately found himself famous. The writer of these lines, who was a child at the time, remembers dimly the sensation the book produced, and the little shudder with which people alluded to it, as if a peculiar horror were mixed with its attractions. He was too young to read it himself, but its title, upon which he fixed his eyes as the book lay upon the table, had a mysterious charm. He had a vague belief, indeed, that the "letter" in question was one of the documents that come by the post, and it was a source of perpetual wonderment to him that it should be of such an unaccustomed hue. Of course it was difficult to explain to a child the significance of poor Hester Prynne's blood-coloured A. But the mystery was at last partly dispelled by his being taken to see a collection of pictures (the annual exhibition of the National Academy), where he encountered a representation of a pale, handsome woman, in a quaint black dress and a white coif, holding between her knees an elfish-looking little girl, fantastically dressed, and crowned with flowers. Embroidered on the woman's breast was a great crimson A, over which the child's fingers, as she glanced strangely out of the picture, were maliciously playing. I was told that this was Hester Prynne and little Pearl, and that when I grew older I might read their interesting history. But the picture remained vividly imprinted on my mind; I had been vaguely frightened and made uneasy by it; and when, years afterwards, I first read the novel, I seemed to myself to have read it before, and to be familiar with its two strange heroines. I mention this incident simply as an indication of the degree to which the success of *The Scarlet Letter* had made the book what is called an actuality. Hawthorne himself was very modest about it; he wrote to his publisher, when there was a question of his undertaking another novel, that what had given the history of Hester Prynne its "vogue" was simply the introductory chapter. In fact, the publication of *The Scarlet Letter* was in the United States a literary event of the first importance. The book was the finest piece of imaginative writing yet put forth in the country. There was a consciousness of this in the welcome that was given it—a satisfaction in the idea of America having produced a novel that belonged to literature, and to the forefront of it. Something might at last be sent to Europe as exquisite in quality as anything that had been received, and the best of it was that the thing was absolutely American; it belonged to the soil, to the air; it came out of the very heart of New England.

It is beautiful, admirable, extraordinary; it has in the highest degree that merit which I have spoken of as the mark of Hawthorne's best things—an indefinable purity and lightness of conception, a quality which in a work of art affects one in the same way as the absence of grossness does in a human being. His fancy, as I just now said, had evidently brooded over the subject for a long time; the situation to be represented had disclosed itself to him in all its phases. When I say in all its phases, the sentence demands modification; for it is to be remembered that if Hawthorne laid his hand upon the well-worn theme, upon the familiar combination of the wife, the lover, and the husband, it was after all but to one period of the history of these three persons that he attached himself. The situation is the situation after the woman's fault has been committed, and the current of expiation and repentance has set in. In spite of the relation between Hester Prynne and Arthur Dimmesdale, no story of love was surely ever less of a "love story." To Hawthorne's imagination the fact that these two persons had loved each other too well was of an interest comparatively vulgar; what appealed to him was the idea of their moral situation in the long years that were to follow. The story, indeed, is in a secondary degree that of Hester Prynne; she becomes, really, after the first scene, an accessory figure; it is not upon her the *dénoûment* depends. It is upon her guilty lover that the author projects most frequently the cold, thin rays of his fitfully-moving lantern, which makes here and there a little luminous circle, on the edge of which hovers the livid and sinister figure of the injured and retributive husband. The story goes on, for the most part, between the lover and the husband—the tormented young Puritan minister, who carries the secret of his own lapse from pastoral purity locked up beneath an exterior that commends itself to the reverence of his flock, while he sees the softer partner of his guilt standing in the full glare of exposure and humbling herself to the misery of atonement—between this more wretched and pitiable culprit, to whom dishonour would come as a comfort and the pillory as a relief, and the older, keener, wiser man, who, to obtain satisfaction for the wrong he has suffered, devises the infernally ingenious plan of conjoining himself with his wronger, living with him, living upon him, and while he pretends to minister to his hidden ailment and to sympathise with his pain, revels in his unsuspected knowledge of these things and stimulates them by malignant arts. The attitude of Roger Chillingworth, and the means he takes to compensate himself—these are the highly original elements in the situation that Hawthorne so ingeniously treats. None of his works are so impregnated with that after-sense of the old Puritan consciousness of life to which allusion has so often been made. If, as M. Montégut says, the qualities of his ancestors *filtered* down through generations into his composition, *The Scarlet Letter* was, as it were, the vessel that gathered up the last of the precious drops. And I say this not because the story happens to be of so-called historical cast, to be told of the early days of Massachusetts and of people in steeple-crowned hats and sad-coloured garments. The historical colouring is rather weak than otherwise; there is little elaboration of detail, of the modern realism of research; and the author has made no great point of causing his figures to speak the English of their period. Nevertheless, the book is full of the moral presence of the race that invented Hester's penance—diluted and complicated with other things, but still perfectly recognisable. Puritanism, in a word, is there, not only objectively, as Hawthorne tried to place it there, but subjectively as well. Not, I mean, in his judgment of his characters, in any harshness of prejudice, or in the obtrusion of a moral lesson; but in the very quality of his own vision, in the tone of the picture, in a certain coldness and exclusiveness of treatment.

The faults of the book are, to my sense, a want of reality and an abuse of the fanciful element—of a certain superficial symbolism. The people strike me not as characters, but as representatives, very picturesquely arranged, of a single state of mind; and the interest of the story lies, not in them, but in the situation, which is insistently kept before us, with little progression, though with a great deal, as I have said, of a certain stable variation; and to which they, out of their reality, contribute little that helps it to live and move. I was made to feel this want of reality, this over-ingenuity, of *The Scarlet Letter,* by chancing not long since upon a novel which was read fifty years ago much more than to-day, but which is still worth reading—the story of *Adam Blair,* by John Gibson Lockhart. This interesting and powerful little tale has a great deal of analogy with Hawthorne's novel—quite enough, at least, to suggest a comparison between them; and the comparison is a very interesting one to make, for it speedily leads us to larger considerations than simple resemblances and divergences of plot.

Adam Blair, like Arthur Dimmesdale, is a Calvinistic minister who becomes the lover of a married woman, is overwhelmed with remorse at his misdeed, and makes a public confession of it; then expiates it by resigning his pastoral office and becoming a humble tiller of the soil, as his father had been. The two stories are of about the same length, and each is the masterpiece (putting aside of course, as far as Lockhart is concerned, the *Life of Scott*) of the author. They deal alike with the manners of a rigidly theological society, and even in certain details they correspond. In each of them, between the guilty pair, there is a charming little girl; though I hasten to say that Sarah Blair (who is not the daughter of the heroine, but the legitimate offspring of the hero, a widower) is far from being as brilliant and graceful an apparition as the admirable little Pearl of *The Scarlet Letter.* The main difference between the two tales is the fact that in the American story the husband plays an all-important part, and in the Scottish plays almost none at all. *Adam Blair* is the history of the passion, and *The Scarlet Letter* the history of its sequel; but nevertheless, if one has read the two books at a short interval, it is impossible to avoid confronting them. I confess that a large portion of the interest of *Adam Blair*, to my mind, when once I had perceived that it would repeat in a great measure the situation of *The Scarlet Letter,* lay in noting its difference of tone. It threw into relief the passionless quality of Hawthorne's novel, its element of cold and ingenious fantasy, its elaborate imaginative delicacy. These things do not precisely constitute a weakness in *The Scarlet Letter;* indeed, in a certain way they constitute a great strength; but the absence of a certain something warm and straightforward, a trifle more grossly human and vulgarly natural, which one finds in *Adam Blair,* will always make Hawthorne's tale less touching to a large number of even very intelligent readers, than a love-story told with the robust, synthetic pathos which served Lockhart so well. His novel is not of the first rank (I should call it an excellent second-rate one), but it borrows a charm from the fact that his vigorous, but not strongly imaginative, mind was impregnated with the reality of his subject. He did not always succeed in rendering this reality; the expression is sometimes awkward and poor. But the reader feels that his vision was clear, and his feeling about the matter very strong and rich. Hawthorne's imagination, on the other hand, plays with his theme so incessantly, leads it such a dance through the moon-lighted air of his intellect, that the thing cools off, as it were, hardens and stiffens, and, producing effects much more exquisite, leaves the reader with a sense of having handled a splendid piece of silversmith's work. Lockhart, by means much more vulgar, produces at moments a greater illusion, and satisfies our inevitable desire for something, in the people in whom it is sought to interest us, that shall be of the same pitch and the same continuity with ourselves. Above all, it is interesting to see how the same subject appears to two men of a thoroughly different cast of mind and of a different race. Lockhart was struck with the warmth of the subject that offered itself to him, and Hawthorne with its coldness; the one with its glow, its sentimental interest—the other with its shadow, its moral interest. Lockhart's story is as decent, as severely draped, as *The Scarlet Letter;* but the author has a more vivid sense than appears to have imposed itself upon Hawthorne, of some of the incidents of the situation he describes; his tempted man and tempting woman are more actual and personal; his heroine in especial, though not in the least a delicate or a subtle conception, has a sort of credible, visible, palpable property, a vulgar roundness and relief, which are lacking to the dim and chastened image of Hester Prynne. But I am going too far; I am comparing simplicity with subtlety, the usual with the refined. Each man wrote as his turn of mind impelled him, but each expressed something more than himself. Lockhart was a dense, substantial Briton, with a taste for the concrete, and Hawthorne was a thin New Englander, with a miasmatic conscience.

In *The Scarlet Letter* there is a great deal of symbolism; there is, I think, too much. It is overdone at times, and becomes mechanical; it ceases to be impressive, and grazes triviality. The idea of the mystic A which the young minister finds imprinted upon his breast and eating into his flesh, in sympathy with the embroidered badge that Hester is condemned to wear, appears to me to be a case in point. This suggestion should, I think, have been just made and dropped; to insist upon it and return to it, is to exaggerate the weak side of the subject. Hawthorne returns to it constantly, plays with it, and seems charmed by it; until at last the reader feels tempted to declare that his enjoyment of it is puerile. In the admirable scene, so superbly conceived and beautifully executed, in which Mr. Dimmesdale, in the stillness of the night, in the middle of the sleeping town, feels impelled to go and stand upon the scaffold where his mistress had formerly enacted her dreadful penance, and then, seeing Hester pass along the street, from watching at a sick-bed, with little Pearl at her side, calls them both to come and stand there beside him—in this masterly episode the effect is almost spoiled by the introduction of one of these superficial conceits. What leads up to it is very fine—so fine that I cannot do better than quote it as a specimen of one of the striking pages of the book.

> But before Mr. Dimmesdale had done speaking, a light gleamed far and wide over all the muffled sky. It was doubtless caused by one of those meteors which the night-watcher may so often observe burning out to waste in the vacant regions of the atmosphere. So powerful was its radiance that it thoroughly illuminated the dense medium of cloud, betwixt the sky and earth. The great vault brightened, like the dome of an immense lamp. It showed the familiar scene of the street with the distinctness of mid-day, but also with the awfulness that is always imparted to familiar objects by an unaccustomed light. The wooden houses, with their jutting stories and quaint gable-peaks; the door-steps and thresholds, with the early grass springing up about them; the garden-plots, black with freshly-turned earth; the wheel-track, little worn, and, even in the market-place, margined with green on either side;—all were visible, but with a singularity of aspect that seemed to give another moral interpretation to the things of this world than they had ever borne before. And there stood the minister, with his hand over his heart; and Hester Prynne, with the embroidered letter glimmering on her bosom; and little Pearl, herself a symbol, and the connecting-link between these two. They stood in the noon of that strange and solemn splendour, as if it were the light that is to reveal all secrets, and the daybreak that shall unite all that belong to one another.

That is imaginative, impressive, poetic; but when, almost immediately afterwards, the author goes on to say that "the minister looking upward to the zenith, beheld there the appearance of an immense letter—the letter A—marked out in lines of dull red light," we feel that he goes too far and is in danger of crossing the line that separates the sublime from its intimate neighbour. We are tempted to say that this is not moral tragedy, but physical comedy. In the same way, too much is made of the intimation that Hester's badge had a scorching property, and that if one touched it one would immediately withdraw one's hand. Hawthorne is perpetually looking for images which shall place themselves in picturesque correspondence with the spiritual facts with which he is concerned, and of course the search is of the very essence of poetry. But in such a process discretion is everything, and when the image becomes importunate it is in danger of seeming to stand for nothing more serious than itself. When Hester meets the minister by appointment in the forest, and sits talking with him while little Pearl wanders away and plays by the edge of the brook, the child is represented as at last making her way over to the other side of the woodland stream, and disporting herself there in a manner which makes her mother feel herself "in some indistinct and tantalising manner, estranged from Pearl; as if the child, in her lonely ramble through the forest, had strayed out of the sphere in which she and her mother dwelt together, and was now vainly seeking to return to it." And Hawthorne devotes a chapter to this idea of the child's having, by putting the brook between Hester and herself, established a kind of spiritual gulf, on the verge of which her little fantastic person innocently mocks at her mother's sense of bereavement. This conception belongs, one would say, quite to the lighter order of a story-teller's devices, and the reader hardly goes with Hawthorne in the large development he gives to it. He hardly goes with him either, I think, in his extreme predilection for a small number of vague ideas which are represented by such terms as "sphere" and "sympathies." Hawthorne makes too liberal a use of these two substantives; it is the solitary defect of his style; and it counts as a defect partly because the words in question are a sort of specialty with certain writers immeasurably inferior to himself.

I had not meant, however, to expatiate upon his defects, which are of the slenderest and most venial kind. *The Scarlet Letter* has the beauty and harmony of all original and complete conceptions, and its weaker spots, whatever they are, are not of its essence; they are mere light flaws and inequalities of surface. One can often return to it; it supports familiarity and has the inexhaustible charm and mystery of great works of art. It is admirably written. Hawthorne afterwards polished his style to a still higher degree, but in his later productions—it is almost always the case in a writer's later productions—there is a touch of mannerism. In *The Scarlet Letter* there is a high degree of polish, and at the same time a charming freshness; his phrase is less conscious of itself. His biographer very justly calls attention to the fact that his style was excellent from the beginning; that he appeared to have passed through no phase of learning how to write, but was in possession of his means from the first of his handling a pen. His early tales, perhaps, were not of a character to subject his faculty of expression to a very severe test, but a man who had not Hawthorne's natural sense of language would certainly have contrived to write them less well. This natural sense of language—this turn for saying things lightly and yet touchingly, picturesquely yet simply, and for infusing a gently colloquial tone into matter of the most unfamiliar import, he had evidently cultivated with great assiduity. I have spoken of the anomalous character of his Note-Books—of his going to such pains often to make a record of incidents which either were not worth remembering or could be easily remembered without its aid. But it helps us to understand the Note-Books if we regard them as a literary exercise. They were compositions, as school-boys say, in which the subject was only the pretext, and the main point was to write a certain amount of excellent English. Hawthorne must at least have written a great many of these things for practice, and he must often have said to himself that it was better practice to write about trifles, because it was a greater tax upon one's skill to make them interesting. And his theory was just, for he has almost always made his trifles interesting. In his novels his art of saying things well is very positively tested, for here he treats of those matters among which it is very easy for a blundering writer to go wrong—the subtleties and mysteries of life, the moral and spiritual maze. In such a passage as one I have marked for quotation from *The Scarlet Letter,* there is the stamp of the genius of style.

Hester Prynne, gazing steadfastly at the clergyman, felt a dreary influence come over her, but wherefore or whence she knew not, unless that he seemed so remote from her own sphere and utterly beyond her reach. One glance of recognition she had imagined must needs pass between them. She thought of the dim forest with its little dell of solitude, and love, and anguish, and the mossy tree-trunk, where, sitting hand in hand, they had mingled their sad and passionate talk with the melancholy murmur of the brook. How deeply had they known each other then! And was this the man? She hardly knew him now! He, moving proudly past, enveloped as it were in the rich music, with the procession of majestic and venerable fathers; he, so unattainable in his worldly position, and still more so in that far vista in his unsympathising thoughts, through which she now beheld him! Her spirit sank with the idea that all must have been a delusion, and that vividly as she had dreamed it, there could be no real bond betwixt the clergyman and herself. And thus much of woman there was in Hester, that she could scarcely forgive him—least of all now, when the heavy footstep of their approaching fate might be heard, nearer, nearer, nearer!—for being able to withdraw himself so completely from their mutual world, while she groped darkly, and stretched forth her cold hands, and found him not!

ALFRED KAZIN ON

Moby-Dick
by Herman Melville, 1851

Joseph Conrad, refusing to write a preface to Moby-Dick in 1907, called it a "strained rhapsody with whaling for a subject," an uncomprehending response typical of the period. American critic Alfred Kazin wrote his introduction to the Riverside edition of 1956 in a different critical climate, one in which Melville's great novel had received long overdue recognition as an American classic.

M*oby-Dick* is not only a very big book; it is also a peculiarly full and rich one, and from the very opening it conveys a sense of abundance, of high creative power, that exhilarates and enlarges the imagination. This quality is felt immediately in the style, which is remarkably easy, natural and "American," yet always literary, and which swells in power until it takes on some of the roaring and uncontainable rhythms with which Melville audibly describes the sea. The best description of this style is Melville's own, when he speaks of the "bold and nervous lofty language" that Nantucket whaling captains learn straight from nature. We feel this abundance in heroic types like the Nantucketers themselves, many of whom are significantly named after Old Testament prophets and kings, for these, too, are mighty men, and the mightiest of them all, Captain Ahab, will challenge the very order of the creation itself. This is the very heart of the book—so much so that we come to feel that there is some shattering magnitude of theme before Melville as he writes, that as a writer he had been called to a heroic new destiny.

It is this constant sense of power that constitutes the book's appeal to us, that explains its hold on our attention. *Moby-Dick* is one of those books that try to bring in as much of life as a writer can get both hands on. Melville even tries to create an image of life itself as a ceaseless creation. The book is written with a personal force of style, a passionate learning, a steady insight into our forgotten connections with the primitive. It sweeps everything before it; it gives us the happiness that only great vigor inspires.

If we start by opening ourselves to this abundance and force, by welcoming not merely the story itself, but the manner in which it speaks to us, we shall recognize in this restlessness, this richness, this persistent atmosphere of magnitude, the essential image on which the book is founded. For *Moby-Dick* is not so much a book *about* Captain Ahab's quest for the whale as it is an experience *of* that quest. This is only to say, what we say of any true poem, that we cannot reduce its essential substance to a subject, that we should not intellectualize and summarize it, but that we should recognize that its very force and beauty lie in the way it is conceived and written, in the qualities that flow from its being a unique entity.

In these terms, *Moby-Dick* seems to be far more of a poem than it is a novel, and since it is a narrative, to be an epic, a long poem on a heroic theme, rather than the kind of realistic fiction that we know today. Of course Melville did not deliberately set out to write a formal epic; but half-consciously, he drew upon many of the traditional characteristics of epic in order to realize the utterly original kind of novel *he* needed to write in his time—the spaciousness of theme and subject, the martial atmosphere, the association of these homely and savage materials with universal myths, the symbolic wanderings of the hero, the indispensable strength of such a hero in Captain Ahab. Yet beyond all this, what distinguishes *Moby-Dick* from modern prose fiction, what ties it up with the older, more formal kind of narrative that was once written in verse, is the fact that Melville is not interested in the meanness, the literal truthfulness, the representative slice of life, that we think of as the essence of modern realism. His book has the true poetic emphasis in that the whole story is constantly being meditated and unravelled through a single mind.

"Call me Ishmael," the book begins. This Ishmael is not only a character in the book; he is also the single voice, or rather the single mind, from whose endlessly turning spool of thought the whole story is unwound. It is Ishmael's contemplativeness, his *dreaming,* that articulates the wonder of the seas and the fabulousness of the whale and the terrors of the deep. All that can be meditated and summed up and hinted at, as the reflective essence of the story itself, is given us by Ishmael, who possesses nothing but man's specifically human gift, which is language. It is Ishmael who tries to sum up the whole creation in a single book and yet keeps at the center of it one American whaling voyage. It is Ishmael's gift for speculation that explains the terror we come to feel before the whiteness of the whale; Ishmael's mind that ranges with mad exuberance through a description of all the seas; Ishmael who piles up image after image of "the mightiest animated mass that has survived the flood." It is Ishmael who, in the wonderful chapter on the masthead, embodies for us man as a thinker, whose reveries transcend space and time as he stands watch high above the seas. And of course it is Ishmael, both actually and as the symbol of man, who is the one survivor of the voyage. Yet utterly alone as he is at the end of the book, floating on the Pacific Ocean, he manages, buoyed up on a coffin that magically serves as his life-buoy, to give us the impression that life itself can be honestly confronted only in the loneliness of each human heart. Always it is this emphasis on Ishmael's personal vision, on the richness and ambiguity of all events as the sceptical, fervent, experience-scarred mind of Ishmael feels and thinks them, that gives us, from the beginning, the new kind of book that *Moby-Dick* is. It is a book which is neither a saga, though it deals in large natural forces, nor a *classical* epic, for we feel too strongly the individual who wrote it. It is a book that is at once primitive, fatalistic, and merciless, like the very oldest books, and yet peculiarly personal, like so many twentieth-century novels, in its significant emphasis on the subjective individual consciousness. The book grows out of a single word, "I," and expands until the soul's voyage of this "I" comes to include a great many things that are unseen and unsuspected by most of us. And this material is always tied to Ishmael, who is not merely a witness to the story—someone who happens to be on board the *Pequod*—but the

living and germinating mind who grasps the world in the tentacles
of his thought.

The power behind this "I" is poetical in the sense that everything comes to us through a constant intervention of language instead of being presented flatly. Melville does not wish, as so many
contemporary writers do, to reproduce ordinary life and conventional speech. He seeks the marvellous and the fabulous aspects
that life wears in secret. He exuberantly sees the world through
language—things exist as his words for them—and much of the
exceptional beauty of the book lies in the unusual incidence of
passages that, in the most surprising contexts, are so piercing in
their poetic intensity. But the most remarkable feat of language in
the book is Melville's ability to make us see that man is not a blank
slate passively open to events, but a mind that constantly seeks
meaning in everything it encounters. In Melville the Protestant
habit of moralizing and the transcendental passion for symbolizing
all things as examples of "higher laws" combined to make a mind
that instinctively brought an inner significance to each episode.
Everything in *Moby-Dick* is saturated in a mental atmosphere. Nothing happens for its own sake in this book, and in the midst of the
chase, Ishmael can be seen meditating it, pulling things apart,
drawing out its significant point.

But Ishmael is not just an intellectual observer; he is also very
much in the story. He suffers; he is there. As his name indicates,
he is an estranged and solitary man; his only friend is Queequeg,
a despised heathen from the South Seas. Queequeg, a fellow "iso-
lato" in the smug world of white middle-class Christians, is the
only man who offers Ishmael friendship; thanks to Queequeg, "no
longer my splintered heart and maddened hand were turned against
the wolfish world. This soothing savage had redeemed it." Why
does Ishmael feel so alone? There are background reasons, Melville's
own: his father went bankrupt and then died in debt when Melville
was still a boy. Melville-Ishmael went to sea—"And at first," he
tells us, "this sort of thing is unpleasant enough. It touches one's
sense of honor, particularly if you come of an old established family
in the land." But there is a deeper, a more universal reason for

Ishmael's apartness, and it is one that will strangely make him kin to his daemonic captain, Ahab. For the burden of his thought, the essential cause of his estrangement, is that he cannot come to any conclusion about anything. He feels at home with ships and sailors because for him, too, one journey ends only to begin another; "and a second ended, only begins a third and so on, for ever and for aye. Such is the endlessness, yea, the intolerableness of all earthly effort."

Ishmael is not merely an orphan; he is an exile, searching alone in the wilderness, with a black man for his only friend. He suffers from doubt and uncertainty far more than he does from homelessness. Indeed, this agony of disbelief *is* his homelessness. For him nothing is ever finally settled and decided; he is man, or as we like to think, modern man, cut off from the certainty that was once his inner world. Ishmael no longer has any sure formal belief. All is in doubt, all is in eternal flux, like the sea. And so condemned, like "all his race from Adam down," to wander the seas of thought, far from Paradise, he now searches endlessly to put the whole broken story together, to find a meaning, to ascertain—where but in the ceaselessness of human thought?—"the hidden cause we seek." Ishmael does not perform any great actions, as Ahab does; he is the most insignificant member of the fo'c'sle and will get the smallest share of the take. But his inner world of thought is almost unbearably symbolic, for he must think, and think, and think, in order to prove to himself that there is a necessary connection between man and the world. He pictures his dilemma in everything he does on board the ship, but never so clearly as when he is shown looking at the sea, searching a meaning to existence from the inscrutable waters.

What Melville did through Ishmael, then, was to put man's distinctly modern feeling of "exile," of abandonment, directly at the center of his stage. For Ishmael there are no satisfactory conclusions to anything; no final philosophy is ever possible. All that man owns in this world, Ishmael would say, is his insatiable mind. This is why the book opens on a picture of the dreaming contemplativeness of mind itself: men tearing themselves loose from their jobs to stand "like silent sentinels all around the town . . . thousands of mortal men fixed in ocean reveries." Narcissus was bemused by that image which "we ourselves see in all rivers and oceans," and this, says Ishmael when he is most desperate, is all that man ever finds when he searches the waters—a reflection of himself. All is inconclusive, restless, an endless flow. And Melville's own style rises to its highest level not in the neo-Shakespearean speeches of Ahab, which are sometimes bombastic, but in those amazing prose flights on the whiteness of the whale and on the Pacific where Ishmael reproduces, in the rhythms of the prose itself, man's brooding interrogation of nature.

II

But Ishmael is a witness not only to his own thoughts, but also a witness to the actions of Captain Ahab. The book is not only a great skin of language stretched to fit the world of man's philosophic wandering; it is also a world of moral tyranny and violent action, in which the principal actor is Ahab. With the entry of Ahab a harsh new rhythm enters the book, and from now on two rhythms—one reflective, the other forceful—alternate to show us the world in which man's thinking and man's doing each follows its own law, Ishmael's thought consciously extends itself to get behind the world of appearances; he wants to see and to understand everything. Ahab's drive is to *prove,* not to discover; the world that tortures Ishmael by its horrid vacancy has tempted Ahab into thinking that he can make it over. He seeks to dominate nature, to impose and to inflict his will on the outside world—whether it be the crew that must jump to his orders or the great white whale that is essentially indifferent to him. As Ishmael is all rumination, so Ahab is all will. Both are thinkers, the difference being that Ishmael thinks as a bystander, has identified his own state with man's utter unimportance in nature. Ahab, by contrast, actively seeks the whale in order to assert man's supremacy over what swims before him as "the monomaniac incarnation" of a superior power:

"If man will strike, strike through the mask! How can the prisoner reach outside except by thrusting through the wall? To me, the white whale is that wall, shoved near to me. Sometimes I think there's naught beyond. But 'tis enough. He tasks me; he heaps me; I see in him outrageous strength, with an inscrutable malice sinewing it. That inscrutable thing is chiefly what I hate; and be the white whale agent, or be the white whale principal, I will wreak that hate upon him. Talk not to me of blasphemy, man; I'd strike the sun if it insulted me. For could the sun do that, then could I do the other; since there is ever a sort of fair play herein, jealousy presiding over all creations. But not my master, man, is even that fair play. Who's over me? Truth hath no confines."

This is Ahab's quest—and Ahab's magnificence. For in this speech Ahab expresses more forcibly than Ishmael ever could, something of the impenitent anger against the universe that all of us can feel. Ahab may be a mad sea captain, a tyrant of the quarter deck who disturbs the crew's sleep as he stomps along on his wooden leg. But this Ahab does indeed speak for all men who, as Ishmael confesses in the frightening meditation on the whiteness of the whale, suspect that "though in many of its aspects this visible world seems formed in love, the invisible spheres were formed in fright." So man, watching the sea heaving around him, sees it as a mad steed that has lost its rider, and looking at his own image in the water, is tortured by the thought that man himself may be an accident, of no more importance in this vast oceanic emptiness than one of Ahab's rare tears dropped into the Pacific.

To the degree that we feel this futility in the face of a blind impersonal nature that "heeds us not," and storm madly, like Ahab, against the dread that there's "naught beyond"—to this extent all men may recognize Ahab's bitterness, his unrelentingness, his inability to rest in that uncertainty which, Freud has told us, modern man must learn to endure. Ahab figures in a symbolic fable; he is acting out thoughts which we all share. But Ahab, even more, is a hero; we cannot insist enough on that. Melville believed in the heroic and he specifically wanted to cast his hero on American lines—someone noble by nature, not by birth, who would have "not the dignity of kings and robes, but that abounding dignity which has no robed investiture." Ahab sinned against man and God, and like his namesake in the Old Testament, becomes a "wicked king." But Ahab is not just a fanatic who leads the whole crew to their destruction; he is a hero of thought who is trying, by terrible force, to reassert man's place in nature. And it is the struggle that Ahab incarnates that makes him so magnificent a *voice*, thundering in Shakespearean rhetoric, storming at the gates of the inhuman, silent world. Ahab is trying to give man, in one awful, final assertion that his will *does* mean something, a feeling of relatedness with his world.

Ahab's effort, then, is to reclaim something that man knows he has lost. Significantly, Ahab proves by the bitter struggle he has to wage that man is fighting in an unequal contest; by the end of the book Ahab abandons all his human ties and becomes a complete fanatic. But Melville has no doubt—nor should we!—that Ahab's quest is *humanly* understandable. And the quest itself supplies the book with its technical *raison d'être*. For it leads us through all the seas and around the whole world; it brings us past ships of every nation. Always it is Ahab's drive that makes up the *passion* of *Moby-Dick,* a passion that is revealed in the descriptive chapters on the whale, whale-fighting, whale-burning, on the whole gory and fascinating industrial process aboard ship that reduces the once proud whale to oil-brimming barrels in the hold. And this passion may be defined as a passion of longing, of hope, of striving: a passion that starts from the deepest loneliness that man can know. It is the great cry of man who feels himself exiled from his "birthright, the merry May-day gods of old," who looks for a new god "to enthrone . . . again in the now egotistical sky; in the now unhaunted hill." The cry is Ahab's—"Who's to doom, when the judge himself is dragged to the bar?"

Behind Ahab's cry is the fear that man's covenant with God has been broken, that there is no purpose to our existence. The *Pequod* is condemned by Ahab to sail up and down the world in search of —a symbol. But this search, mad as it seems to Starbuck the first mate, who is a Christian, nevertheless represents Ahab's real humanity. For the ancient covenant is never quite broken so long as man still thirsts for it. And because Ahab, as Melville intended him to, represents the aristocracy of intellect in our democracy, because he seeks to transcend the limitations that good conventional men like Starbuck, philistine materialists like Stubb, and unthinking fools like Flask want to impose on everybody else, Ahab speaks for the humanity that belongs to man's imaginative vision of himself.

Yet with all this, we must not forget that Ahab's quest takes place, unceasingly, in a very practical world of whaling, as part of the barbaric and yet highly necessary struggle by man to support himself physically in nature. It is this that gives the book its primitive vitality, its burning authenticity. For *Moby-Dick*, it must be emphasized, is not simply a symbolic fable; nor, as we have already seen, can it possibly be construed as simply a "sea story." It is the story of agonizing thought in the midst of brutal action, of thought that questions every action, that annuls it from within, as it were—but that cannot, in this harsh world, relieve man of the fighting, skinning, burning, the back-breaking row to the whale, the flying harpoons, the rope that can take you off "voicelessly as Turkish mutes bowstring their victims." *Moby-Dick* is a representation of the passionate mind speaking, for its metaphysical concerns, out of the very midst of life. So, after the first lowering, Queequeg is shown sitting all night in a submerged boat, holding up a lantern like an "imbecile candle in the heart of that almighty forlornness . . . the sign and symbol of a man without hope, hopelessly holding up hope in the midst of despair." Melville insists that our thinking is *not* swallowed up by practical concerns, that man constantly searches for a reality equal to his inner life of thought —and it is his ability to show this in the midst of a brutal, dirty whaling voyage that makes *Moby-Dick* such an astonishing book. Just as Ahab is a hero, so *Moby-Dick* itself is a heroic book. What concerns Melville is not merely the heroism that gets expressed in physical action, but the heroism of thought itself as it rises above its seeming insignificance and proclaims, in the very teeth of a seemingly hostile and malevolent creation, that man's voice *is* heard for something against the watery waste and the deep, that man's thought has an echo in the universe.

III

This is the quest. But what makes *Moby-Dick* so fascinating, and in a sense even uncanny, is that the issue is always in doubt, and remains so to the end. Melville was right when he wrote to Hawthorne: "I have written a wicked book, and feel as spotless as the lamb." And people who want to construe *Moby-Dick* into a condemnation of mad, bad Ahab will always miss what Melville meant when he wrote of his book: "It is not a piece of fine feminine Spitalfields silk—but it is of the horrible texture of a fabric that should be woven of ships' cables & hawsers. A Polar wind blows through it, & birds of prey hover over it." For in the struggle between man's effort to find meaning in nature, and the indifference of nature itself, which simply eludes him (nature here signifies the whole external show and force of animate life in a world suddenly emptied of God, one where an "intangible malignity" has reigned from the beginning), Melville often portrays the struggle from the side of nature itself. He sees the whale's view of things far more than he does Ahab's: and Moby-Dick's milk-white head, the tail feathers of the sea birds streaming from his back like pennons, are described with a rapture that is like the adoration of a god. Even in the most terrible scenes of the shark massacre, where the sharks bend around like bows to bite at their own entrails, or in the ceaseless motion of "my dear Pacific," the "Potters' fields of all four continents," one feels that Melville is transported by the naked reality of things, the great unending flow of the creation itself, where the great shroud of the sea rolls over the doomed ship "as it rolled five thousand years ago." Indeed, one feels in the end that it is only the necessity to keep one person alive as a witness to the story that saves Ishmael from the general ruin and wreck. In Melville's final vision of the whole, it is not fair but it is entirely *just* that the whale should destroy the ship, that man should be caught up on the beast. It is just in a cosmic sense, not in the sense that the prophet (Father Mapple) predicts the punishment of man's disobedience in the telling of Jonah's story from the beginning, where the point made is the classic reprimand of God to man when He speaks out of the whirlwind. What Melville does is to speak for the whirlwind, for the watery waste, for the sharks.

It is this that gives *Moby Dick* its awful and crushing power. It is a unique gift. Goethe said that he wanted, as a writer, to know what it is like to be a woman. But Melville sometimes makes you feel that he knows, as a writer, what it is like to be the eyes of the rock, the magnitude of the whale, the scalding sea, the dreams that lie buried in the Pacific. It is all, of course, seen through human eyes—yet there is in Melville a cold, final, ferocious hopelessness, a kind of ecstatic masochism, that delights in punishing man, in heaping coals on his head, in drowning him. You see it in the scene of the whale running through the herd with an open harpoon in his body, cutting down his own; in the sharks eating at their own entrails and voiding from them in the same convulsion; in the terrible picture of Pip the cabin boy jumping out of the boat in fright and left on the Pacific to go crazy; in Queequeg falling into the "honey head" of the whale; in the ropes that suddenly whir up from the spindles and carry you off; in the final awesome picture of the whale butting its head against the *Pequod*. In all these scenes there is an ecstasy in horror, the horror of nature in itself, nature "pure," without God or man: the void. It is symbolized by the whiteness of the whale, the whiteness that is not so much a color as the absence of color. "Is it that by its indefiniteness it shadows forth the heartless voids and immensities of the universe, and thus stabs us from behind with the thought of annihilation, when beholding the white depths of the milky way?" And it is this picture of existence as one where man has only a peep-hole on the mystery itself, that constitutes the most remarkable achievement of Melville's genius. For as in the meditation on the whiteness of the whale, it becomes an uncanny attempt to come to grips with nature as it might be conceived with man entirely left out; or, what amounts to the same thing, with man losing his humanity and being exclusively responsive to primitive and racial memories, to the trackless fathomless nothing that has been from the beginning, to the very essence of a beginning that, in contradiction to all man's scriptures, had no divine history, no definite locus, but just *was*—with man slipped into the picture much later.

This view of reality, this ability to side with nature rather than with man, means an ability to love what has no animation, what is inhumanly still, what is not in search, as man himself is—a hero running against time and fighting against "reality." Here Melville puts, as it were, his ear to reality itself: to the rock rather than to the hero trying to get his sword out of the rock. He does it by constantly, and bitterly, and savagely, in fact, comparing man with the great thing he is trying to understand. Ahab may be a hero by trying to force himself on what is too much for him, but Melville has no doubt that man is puny and presumptuous and easily overwhelmed—in short, drowned—in the great storm of reality he tries to encompass.

This sense of scale lies behind the chapters on the natural history of the whale, and behind the constant impressing on our minds of the contrast between man and the whale—man getting into a small boat, man being overwhelmed by his own weapons. The greatest single metaphor in the book is that of bigness, and even when Melville laughs at himself for trying to hook this Leviathan with a pen—"Bring me a condor's quill! Bring me Vesuvius' crater for an inkstand!"—we know that he not merely feels exhilaration at attempting this mighty subject, but that he is also abashed, he feels grave; mighty waters are rolling around him. This compelling sense of magnitude, however, gets him to organize the book brilliantly, in a great flood of chapters—some of them very small, one or two only a paragraph long, in the descriptive method which is the great homage that he pays to his subject, and which so provides him with an inexhaustible delight in devoting himself to every conceivable detail about the whale. And, to go back to a theme mentioned earlier, it is this sense of a limitless subject that gives the style its peculiarly loping quality, as if it were constantly looking for connectives, since on the subject of the whale no single word or statement is enough. But these details tend, too, to heap up in such a staggering array as to combine into the awesomeness of a power against which Ahab's challenge is utterly vain, and against which his struggle to show his superiority over the ordinary processes of nature becomes blasphemous. The only thing left to man, Melville seems to tell us, is to take the span of this magnitude—to feel and to record the power of this mighty torrent, this burning fire.

And it is this, this poetic power, rather than any specifically human one, this power of transcription rather than of any alteration of life that will admit human beings into its tremendous scale, that makes up the greatness of the book—by giving us the measure of Melville's own relation to the nature that his hero so futilely attempts to master or defy. For though Melville often takes a grim and almost cruel pleasure in showing man tumbling over before the magnitude of the universe, and though much of the book is concerned, as in the sections on fighting and "cooking" the whale, with man's effort to get a grip on external nature, first through physical assault and then by scientific and industrial cunning, man finds his final relatedness to nature neither as a hero (Ahab) nor by heeding Father Mapple's old prophetic warning of man's proper subservience to God. Though all his attempted gains from nature fail him, and all goes down with the *Pequod*—all man's hopes of profit, of adjustment to orthodoxy (Starbuck), even of the wisdom that is in madness (Pip)—man, though forever alien to the world, an Ishmael, is somehow in tune with it, with its torrential rhythms, by dint of his art, by the directness with which his words grasp the world, by the splendor of his perceptions, by the lantern which he holds up "like a candle in the midst of the almighty forlornness." Man is not merely a waif in the world; he is an ear listening to the sea that almost drowns him; an imagination, a mind, that hears the sea in the shell, and darts behind all appearance to the beginning of things, and runs riot with the frightful force of the sea itself. There, in man's incredible and unresting mind, is the fantastic gift with which we enter into what is not our own, what is even against us—and for this, so amazingly, we can speak.

ANTHONY BURGESS ON

Uncle Tom's Cabin
by Harriet Beecher Stowe, 1852

Wildly successful and influential in the pre-Civil War days of the mid-nineteenth century, Uncle Tom's Cabin *has become a kind of cultural artifact no longer taken seriously as a work of art. In an essay originally published in* Encounter *in 1966 under the title, "Making de White Boss Frown," Anthony Burgess attempts to revise our notions of what he considers a neglected masterpiece.*

Sentimental and didactic, sub-Dickens with the American South as one big Dotheboys Hall (though no satisfying thrashing of Squeers-Legree), *Uncle Tom's Cabin* expended its ration of serious attention in its own day, leaving the slush and not the anger for posterity. That is the general view, at least in England. American organs like the *Bulletin of the Historical and Philosophical Society of Ohio* can produce scholarly papers like "Eliza Crossing the Ice—A Reappraisal of Sources," and students of the Civil War—like Edmund Wilson in *Patriotic Gore*—accord it the attention due to any book that helped to change history. Only in the USSR, whose bookshops parade it next to *Three Men in a Boat, Hatter's Castle,* and the novels of Messrs. Braine and Sillitoe, is it still purveyed as a piece of literary socialist realism, a device of confirmation. But, if we are to take seriously the literature of the South, from Mark Twain to Faulkner, and if we are to accept that our own age shows the true flowering of the novel of protest, we cannot afford to neglect Mrs. Stowe, who was the mother of both.

"The little woman who made this great war"—so proudly she was hailed by President Lincoln in 1862. She didn't, in fact, quite make it, but she made it possible for the making of it to seem the

4 9

only way out of the North-South impasse. First serialised in the abolitionist *National Era,* her masterpiece came out as a book in 1852, two years after the Compromise which satisfied no one but held off war for a decade. Though California entered the Union as a free state, that Compromise did not expressly forbid the extension of Negro slavery to the territories gained from the Mexican War, but neither did it condone expansion of so lucrative a trade and so restful an institution. Southern acceptance of the Compromise depended on how far the North was willing to enforce the Fugitive Slave Law: men north of the Ohio had to dull their consciences to keep the peace and the Union. *Uncle Tom's Cabin* appeared as a whetstone; it did not argue, it showed. There was the brilliantly articulate escaped slave George, prototype of James Baldwin but far handsomer and not so black: walnut-juiced to temper the Euro-African yellow, he could be taken, in his Italianate cloak and with his brace of pistols, as some Byronic rebel wholly acceptable to the ladies' reading circles of Concord; there was his wife Eliza, palely beautiful with a beautiful child, running, by God's grace, over the ice-blocks of the Ohio. No more sympathetic refugees could well be imagined. Southern readers picked up a Scott-looking romance ("Late in the afternoon of a chilly day in February, two gentlemen were sitting alone over their wine, in a well-furnished dining parlour, in the town of P—, in Kentucky") and found that what they had there was a bitter attack on a constitutional right; their anger helped to sell three hundred thousand copies of the American edition in the first year alone. *Uncle Tom's Cabin* helped to start the crumbling of the 1850 Compromise and to show that no further one was possible. In that sense it did what Lincoln claimed it did.

Apart from a literary style that recalls (and probably influenced) the phthisic Sunday-school prizes which reconciled working-class children to malnutrition and a premature transfiguration, *Uncle Tom's Cabin* has been chiefly neglected—in our own age—because it is hard to accept that an instrument of historical change should also be a work of art. The Victorian men of letters who were also liberals had to swallow *Uncle Tom's Cabin* whole without meanly regurgitating the style. But the book's popularity soon made it possible to discount the literary content altogether. It was eaten in fragments—tract-abridgements, school-selections, dramatic adaptations. As a barnstorming melodrama on tour (little Eva dragged heavenwards on a pulley), as a silent film (accompanied by the tunes of Stephen Foster), it held a large public till late in the nineteen-twenties. Even in Catholic Lancashire, where I was brought up, it was part of the pop-art of childhood, though the Church had placed it on the *Index* and enfranchisement had raised the price of cotton in our grandfathers' hard times. The vitality of the work is considerable. It survived its debasement as a bogus Siamese *wayang* in *The King and I*, recalling that Anna Leonowens had written to Mrs. Stowe about the Lady Sonn Klean's liberating all her slaves, saying: "I am wishful to be good like Harriet Beecher Stowe, and never again to buy human bodies, but only to let them go free once more." Now, it seems, we have to take the whole book again, since there is little relevant to our age that can be taken out of it. Today's Negroes, who reject martyrdom and intend to overcome, are ashamed of bible-thumbing Uncle Tom; George Harris, prophet of a vital Africa, has become a demagogue with two gold Cadillacs. If the book is to mean anything now, a good deal of the meaning must reside in the art.

Reading it, we find that all we have to forgive is the style. This is an un-American activity, a cluster of fashionable importations—chiefly from Scott and Dickens, though, in the Simon Legree episodes, Mrs. Stowe draws on that earlier Gothic which continues, in more sophisticated forms, to exert its appeal for Americans. Structurally, the book is very sound, and it even has a visual skeleton provided by the geography of slavery. Kentucky is the middle earth, a vale of tears but with the Jordan-Ohio as its north frontier, Canaan—Illinois, Indiana, or Ohio—on the other side. Then come the Great Lakes and the haven of Canada. George and Eliza make the journey and, in freedom, George is able to deliver a manifesto on the secular glory of a new Africa. "I go to Liberia," he says, "not as to an Elysium of romance, but as to *a field of work*." And Mrs. Stowe comments: "If we are not mistaken, the world will yet hear from him there." As for Uncle Tom, who has the other half of the story, his way lies south from Kentucky, down the Mississippi to the precarious earthly paradise of New Orleans, then northwest to martyrdom on the Red River. He has no Liberia to look forward to, only the Christian heaven.

What may look like self-indulgence frequently turns out to be structural necessity. The death of little Eva, whom Tom saved from drowning, thus earning a cushy billet with the St. Clare family, is usually picked out as the limit in slush: "A bright, a glorious smile passed over her face, and she said, brokenly,—'O! love,—joy,—peace!' gave one sigh and passed from death unto life!" But the image of a good Christian death is what sustains Tom when he is suffering not from phthisis but from Simon Legree. Lashed first to labour and at last to death, Tom needs Eva to keep him steady in belief and resolve, a sort of animated hagiograph. The sugar lilies and the weeping Topsy may be intolerable, but Mrs. Stowe makes up for that—Faulknerian realism begins here—with those protracted sufferings on the old plantation. There is, anyway, a balance, no gratuitous feeding (as so often in Dickens) of a necrophagous appetite. As for Tom's forgiving Christianity—"O, Mas'r! don't bring this great sin on your soul! It will hurt you more than 't will me! Do the worst you can, my troubles'll be over soon"—it doesn't deserve the sneers of the Negro intellectuals, or white ones either. What palliative ought a progressive slavery novel to make available to the victims of Legree—a bundle of abolitionist pamphlets, gems from Tom Paine? The visions of secular reform have always been the real pie in the sky; a man entering the gas chamber needs heaven. What may have disturbed Christians in Mrs. Stowe's own day—apart from cries like "Oh my country! these things are done under the shadow of thy laws! O, Christ, thy church sees them, almost in silence!"—is the implication that Christianity only really works as a slave religion.

*   *   *

Even in his hammiest postures as a slave with a soul, Tom is totally convincing. Indeed, all Mrs. Stowe's characters, who might well have been mere morality fascias, have a remarkable roundness—even the "good" master Shelby, whose implausible sale of Tom and Eliza's child sets the plot working. Her triumph is Augustine St. Clare, the indolent and indulgent New Orleans gentleman who lets his Negro butler bully him and Tom preach his hind leg off. Attractive as he is, Mrs. Stowe doesn't hide from us that his paternalism is as misguided as Legree's proprietorialism is vicious. St. Clare's slaves are, for the most part, a great deal happier than many a free-born white, but his free and easy welfare state cannot, and does not, survive his death in a café fracas. Tom has been promised his manumission (it is only a matter of asking), but the papers are still unsigned when St. Clare dies, and Tom is sold down the river. St. Clare has made the mistake of assuming that personal benevolence can turn bad law into good; but, in effect, good law comes to mean no law at all, and without law we are, however paternally coddled, wholly vulnerable. As for benevolence, that is precisely well-wishing, not acting. For all his weaknesses, St. Clare is a sort of voice of history; he knows perfectly well that the slave-owning mentality is not confined to the Southern States of America. How about the British labourer? His New England cousin, Miss Ophelia, will not have it that British factories are another kind of plantation: "The English labourer is not sold, traded, parted from his family, whipped." St. Clare replies:

> "He is as much at the will of his employer as if he were sold to him. The slave-owner can whip his refractory slave to death,—the capitalist can starve him to death. As to family security, it is hard to say which is the worst,—to have one's children sold, or see them starve to death at home."

American slavery is no more than

> the more bold and palpable infringement of human rights; actually buying a man up, like a horse,—looking at his teeth, cracking his joints, and

trying his paces, and then paying down for him,—having speculators, breeders, traders, and brokers in human bodies and souls,—sets the thing before the eyes of the civilised world in a more tangible form, though the thing done be, after all, in its nature, the same; that is, appropriating one set of human beings to the use and improvement of another, without any regard to their own.

It is St. Clare, more than the Northern abolitionists, who sees that a *"dies irae"* is coming everywhere. Like any Marxist, he regards the process as ineluctable, but he is an aristocrat who calls himself a democrat and feels neither regret nor elation at the impending change in the order. He plays the *Dies Irae* from Mozart's *Requiem* on the piano, pushing back his very prophecy into an art that serves a religion he cannot accept, despite Tom's humble but importunate evangelising. It is as complex a portrait as any in nineteenth-century fiction.

Mrs. Stowe's resistance to the technique of the morality (a far stronger resistance than is evinced in much present-day protest literature—Baldwin's *Blues for Mister Charlie,* for instance) is attested by the divisions built into her characters. Miss Ophelia has a New Englander's abhorrence of Southern slavery, but also of the slackness, the reversion to tropical torpor, which her cousin's indulgence seems to encourage. She wants Negroes to be Christianised into the austere patterns of the North, educated and turned into free wage-earning Americans, but (and here her crime is, in its way, as great as that of the slave-owners) she cannot bear the touch of a black skin. Paradoxically, to be surrounded by slaves may be a means of accepting them as a sort of human beings; it will rarely—since these black bodies are your property—mean physical revulsion. The attitudinising of the North, the work of enlightenment delegated to missionaries, will not do; Miss Ophelia (whom the slaves, with prophetic insight, call Miss Feely) must learn to cherish dark flesh with her own hands. That is why Topsy is brought in, Miss Ophelia's own charge and passive, or resistant, educatrix; eventually she will be taken to New England as a living witness that Negroes are real touchable people.

The whole book sometimes seems to resolve itself into a protest, not just against slavery, but against the forces—law or prejudice—which destroy simple affection or break family ties. The real horror of slavery is that it separates mothers from their children: it is a horror that Mrs. Stowe, a bereaved mother, is qualified to express: no amount of abstract, diffused abhorrence of slavery—appropriate to a male writer—could have given *Uncle Tom's Cabin* its peculiar bitterness. And yet the book is far from being a mere monothematic exercise, and that is where much of its distinction lies. We are given a picture of mid-nineteenth-century America which is as cosy as Mrs. Gaskell's England: tea is taken, chicken pie is cooked, the crinolined ladies are subject to the vapours, the calm legislative processes go on in the capital. But a system is accepted which is more than mere hypocrisy. Hypocrisy is allegiance to the letter and denial of the spirit; in the American South the letter itself has to admit ambiguous values. There are men and women to whom, since they are only chattels, Christian institutions cannot apply. One of the most sickening episodes in the book is the recollection of the marriage between George and Eliza, sentimentally arranged by Mrs. Shelby with all the bijou trimmings, presided over by a real clergyman. But this marriage can mean nothing, since slaves are sold as individual bodies: the slave family just does not exist. Mrs. Stowe will allow husbands to be separated from wives, but the wresting of a child from its mother cannot be tolerated by nature: the mother will kill herself, escape with her child (but only, as with Eliza, through a kind of miracle) or—improbably, as in the denouement of the book—achieve reunion in freedom. It is through the disruption of nature that slavery is shown as not merely evil but mad.

Mrs. Stowe is prophetic in that she implies no real hope for the integration of the races in America. The future of the Negro lies in Africa, and the future of the world may lie there too:

> In that far-off mystic land of gold, and gems, and spices, and waving palms, and wondrous flowers, and miraculous fertility, will awake new forms of art, new styles of splendour; and the Negro race, no longer despised and trodden down, will, perhaps, show forth some of the latest and most magnificent revelations of human life. Certainly they will, in

their gentleness, their lowly docility of heart, their aptitude to repose on
a superior mind and rest on a higher power, their childlike simplicity of
affection, and facility of forgiveness. . . . Perhaps, as God chasteneth
whom he loveth, he hath chosen poor Africa in the furnace of affliction,
to make her the highest and noblest in that kingdom which he will set
up, when every other kingdom has been tried, and failed; for the first
shall be last, and the last first.

It is straight from Revelations, the Holy City, with no tse-tse flies
or dysentery; it's the other side of the Jordan, no more. Charles
Dickens, for one, would not have it:

I doubt there being any warrant for making out the African race to
be a great race, or for supposing the future destinies of the world to lie
in that direction; and I think this extreme championship likely to repel
some useful sympathy and support.

And certainly, since only Uncle Tom looks "respectable enough to
be a Bishop of Carthage" and only George Harris shows any intelligence, the rest of Mrs. Stowe's Negroes exhibiting few of the
virtues of a God-chosen race, we find it hard to reconcile the prophet
with the novelist.

It is the novelist who counts. Mrs. Stowe's primary gift to Southern
fiction derives from an ability to take the Negro seriously as subject-
matter, and to render—for the first time—the involutions of the
Negro character through exact transcription of speech. Mrs. Shelby's Sam, sent out to "help this yer Mas'r to cotch Lizy," explains
why he hindered instead:

"Dat ar was *conscience,* Andy; when I thought of gwine arter Lizy,
I railly spected Mas'r was sot dat way. When I found Missis was sot the
contrar, dat ar was conscience *more yet*—cause fellers allers gets more
by stickin' to Missis' side,—so yer see I's persistent either way, and
sticks up to conscience, and holds on to principles. Yes, *principles,*" said
Sam, giving an enthusiastic toss to a chicken's neck,—"what's principles
good for, if we isn't persistent, I wanter know? Thar, Andy, you may
have dat ar bone,—'tan't picked quite clean."

The speech is the speech of a whole tradition of fictional Negroes,
not excluding film and music-hall, but the argument is that of the

modern African politician. And here is the voice of modern Negro
protest:

> ". . . What country have *I*, or any one like me, born of slave mothers?
> What laws are there for us? We don't make them,—we don't consent
> to them,—we have nothing to do with them; all they do for us is to crush
> us, and keep us down. Haven't I heard your Fourth-of-July speeches?
> Don't you tell us, once a year, that governments derive their just power
> from the consent of the governed? Can't a fellow *think,* that hears such
> things? Can't he put this and that together, and see what it comes to?"

It is the impact of the characters, and what they say, that
excuses the frequent ineptitude of the *récit,* the hollow prophecies,
and the tedious moralising. *Uncle Tom's Cabin* works well as fiction,
but the fiction is also the feather of the dart. It has, whether we
have read it or not, done more than any work of literature to make
Negro servitude in the South seem not only the type of all slavery
but the only one we ought to feel guilty about. We can forget what
happened to the Jews, or what is still going on under Islam, or that
a greater white novelist than Mrs. Stowe was a galley-slave. Thanks
to her, colour has become for all time the colour of the oppressed.

The Adventures of Huckleberry Finn
by Samuel L. Clemens (Mark Twain), 1885

Like his fellow Missourian Mark Twain, T. S. Eliot grew up beside the Mississippi River, an experience that Eliot once called "incommunicable" to those who haven't had it. In this introduction to a British edition, the sixty-two-year-old writer culls upon memories of his own boyhood half a century after Twain's to illuminate the genius of Huckleberry Finn.

The Adventures of Huckleberry Finn
is the only one of Mark Twain's various books which can be called
a masterpiece. I do not suggest that it is his only book of permanent
interest; but it is the only one in which his genius is completely
realized, and the only one which creates its own category. There
are pages in *Tom Sawyer* and in *Life on the Mississippi* which are,
within their limits, as good as anything with which one can compare
them in *Huckleberry Finn;* and in other books there are drolleries
just as good of their kind. But when we find one book by a prolific
author which is very much superior to all the rest, we look for
the peculiar accident or concourse of accidents which made that
book possible. In the writing of *Huckleberry Finn* Mark Twain
had two elements which, when treated with his sensibility and
his experience, formed a great book: these two are the Boy and
the River.

Huckleberry Finn is, no doubt, a book which boys enjoy. I cannot
speak from memory: I suspect that a fear on the part of my parents
lest I should acquire a premature taste for tobacco, and perhaps
other habits of the hero of the story, kept the book out of my way.
But *Huckleberry Finn* does not fall into the category of juvenile
fiction. The opinion of my parents that it was a book unsuitable

for boys left me, for most of my life, under the impression that it was a book suitable only for boys. Therefore it was only a few years ago that I read for the first time, and in that order, *Tom Sawyer* and *Huckleberry Finn*.

Tom Sawyer did not prepare me for what I was to find its sequel to be. *Tom Sawyer* seems to me to be a boys' book, and a very good one. The River and *the* Boy make their appearance in it; the narrative is good; and there is also a very good picture of society in a small mid-Western river town (for St. Petersburg is more Western than Southern) a hundred years ago. But the point of view of the narrator is that of an adult observing a boy. And Tom is the ordinary boy, though of quicker wits, and livelier imagination, than most. Tom is, I suppose, very much the boy that Mark Twain had been: he is remembered and described as he seemed to his elders, rather than created. Huck Finn, on the other hand, is the boy that Mark Twain still was, at the time of writing his adventures. We look at Tom as the smiling adult does: Huck we do not look at—we see the world through his eyes. The two boys are not merely different types; they were brought into existence by different processes. Hence in the second book their roles are altered. In the first book Huck is merely the humble friend—almost a variant of the traditional valet of comedy; and we see him as he is seen by the conventional respectable society to which Tom belongs, and of which, we feel sure, Tom will one day become an eminently respectable and conventional member. In the second book their nominal relationship remains the same; but here it is Tom who has the secondary role. The author was probably not conscious of this, when he wrote the first two chapters: *Huckleberry Finn* is not the kind of story in which the author knows, from the beginning, what is going to happen. Tom then disappears from our view; and when hc returns, he has only two functions. The first is to provide a foil for Huck. Huck's persisting admiration for Tom only exhibits more clearly to our eyes the unique qualities of the former and the commonplaceness of the latter. Tom has the imagination of a lively boy who has read a good deal of romantic fiction: he might, of course, become a writer—he might become Mark Twain. Or rather, he might become the more commonplace aspect of Mark Twain. Huck has not imagination, in the sense in which Tom has it: he has, instead, vision. He sees the real world; and he does not judge it—he allows it to judge itself.

Tom Sawyer is an orphan. But he has his aunt; he has, as we learn later, other relatives; and he has the environment into which he fits. He is wholly a social being. When there is a secret band to be formed, it is Tom who organizes it and prescribes the rules. Huck Finn is alone: there is no more solitary character in fiction. The fact that he has a father only emphasizes his loneliness; and he views his father with a terrifying detachment. So we come to see Huck himself in the end, as one of the permanent symbolic figures of fiction; not unworthy to take a place with Ulysses, Faust, Don Quixote, Don Juan, Hamlet and other great discoveries that man has made about himself.

It would seem that Mark Twain was a man who—perhaps like most of us—never became in all respects mature. We might even say that the adult side of him was boyish, and that only the boy in him, that was Huck Finn, was adult. As Tom Sawyer grown up, he wanted success and applause (Tom himself always needs an audience). He wanted prosperity, a happy domestic life of a conventional kind, universal approval, and fame. All of these things he obtained. As Huck Finn he was indifferent to all these things; and being a composite of the two, Mark Twain both strove for them, and resented their violation of his integrity. Hence he became the humorist and even clown: with his gifts, a certain way to success, for everyone could enjoy his writings without the slightest feeling of discomfort, self-consciousness or self-criticism. And hence, on the other hand, his pessimism and misanthropy. To be a misanthrope is to be in some way divided; or it is a sign of an uneasy conscience. The pessimism which Mark Twain discharged into *The Man That Corrupted Hadleyburg* and *What is Man?* springs less from observation of society, than from his hatred of himself for allowing society to tempt and corrupt him and give him what he wanted. There is no wisdom in it. But all this personal problem has been diligently examined by Mr. Van Wyck Brooks; and it is not Mark Twain, but *Huckleberry Finn,* that is the subject of this introduction.

You cannot say that Huck himself is either a humorist or a misanthrope. He is the impassive observer: he does not interfere, and, as I have said, he does not judge. Many of the episodes that occur on the voyage down the river, after he is joined by the Duke and the King (whose fancies about themselves are akin to the kind of fancy that Tom Sawyer enjoys) are in themselves farcical; and if it were not for the presence of Huck as the reporter of them, they would be no more than farce. But, seen through the eyes of Huck, there is a deep human pathos in these scoundrels. On the other hand, the story of the feud between the Grangerfords and the Shepherdsons is a masterpiece in itself: yet Mark Twain could not have written it so, with that economy and restraint, with just the right details and no more, and leaving to the reader to make his own moral reflections, unless he had been writing in the person of Huck. And the *style* of the book, which is the style of Huck, is what makes it a far more convincing indictment of slavery than the sensationalist propaganda of *Uncle Tom's Cabin.* Huck is passive and impassive, apparently always the victim of events; and yet, in his acceptance of his world and of what it does to him and others, he is more powerful than his world, because he is more *aware* than any other person in it.

Repeated readings of the book only confirm and deepen one's admiration of the consistency and perfect adaptation of the writing. This is a style which at the period, whether in America or in England, was an innovation, a new discovery in the English language. Other authors had achieved natural speech in relation to particular characters—Scott with characters talking Lowland Scots, Dickens with cockneys: but no one else had kept it up through the whole of a book. Thackeray's Yellowplush, impressive as he is, is an obvious artifice in comparison. In *Huckleberry Finn* there is no exaggeration of grammar or spelling or speech, there is no sentence or phrase to destroy the illusion that these are Huck's own words.

It is not only in the way in which he tells his story, but in the details he remembers, that Huck is true to himself. There is, for instance, the description of the Grangerford interior as Huck sees it on his arrival; there is the list of the objects which Huck and Jim salvaged from the derelict house:

> We got an old tin lantern, and a butcher-knife without any handle, and a bran-new Barlow knife worth two bits in any store, and a lot of tallow candles, and a tin candlestick, and a gourd, and a tin cup, and a ratty old bedquilt off the bed, and a reticule with needles and pins and beeswax and buttons and thread and all such truck in it, and a hatchet and some nails, and a fish-line as thick as my little finger, with some monstrous hooks on it, and a roll of buckskin, and a leather dog-collar, and a horseshoe; and some vials of medicine that didn't have no label on them; and just as we was leaving I found a tolerable good curry-comb, and Jim he found a ratty old fiddle-bow, and a wooden leg. The straps was broke off of it, but barring that, it was a good enough leg, though it was too long for me and not long enough for Jim, and we couldn't find the other one, though we hunted all round.
>
> And so, take it all round, we made a good haul.

This is the sort of list that a boy reader should pore over with delight; but the paragraph performs other functions of which the boy reader would be unaware. It provides the right counterpoise to the horror of the wrecked house and the corpse; it has a grim precision which tells the reader all he needs to know about the way of life of the human derelicts who had used the house; and (especially the wooden leg, and the fruitless search for its mate) reminds us at the right moment of the kinship of mind and the sympathy between the boy outcast from society and the negro fugitive from the injustice of society.

Huck in fact would be incomplete without Jim, who is almost as notable a creation as Huck himself. Huck is the passive observer of men and events, Jim the submissive sufferer from them; and they are equal in dignity. There is no passage in which their relationship is brought out more clearly than the conclusion of the chapter in which, after the two have become separated in the fog, Huck in the canoe and Jim on the raft, Huck, in his impulse of boyish mischief, persuades Jim for a time that the latter had dreamt the whole episode.

> ". . . my heart wuz mos' broke bekase you wuz los', en I didn' k'yer no mo' what become er me en de raf'. En when I wake up en fine you back agin', all safe en soun', de tears come en I could a got down on my knees en kiss' yo' foot, I's so thankful. En all you wuz thinkin' 'bout wuz how you could make a fool uv ole Jim wid a lie. Dat truck dah is *trash*; en trash is what people is dat puts dirt on de head er dey fren's en makes 'em ashamed." . . .
>
> It was fifteen minutes before I could work myself up to go and humble myself to a nigger—but I done it, and I warn't ever sorry for it afterwards, neither.

This passage has been quoted before; and if I quote it again, it is because I wish to elicit from it one meaning that is, I think, usually overlooked. What is obvious in it is the pathos and dignity of Jim, and this is moving enough; but what I find still more disturbing, and still more unusual in literature, is the pathos and dignity of the boy, when reminded so humbly and humiliatingly, that his position in the world is not that of other boys, entitled from time to time to a practical joke; but that he must bear, and bear alone, the responsibility of a man.

It is Huck who gives the book style. The River gives the book its form. But for the River, the book might be only a sequence of adventures with a happy ending. A river, a very big and powerful river, is the only natural force that can wholly determine the course of human peregrination. At sea, the wanderer may sail or be carried by winds and currents in one direction or another; a change of wind or tide may determine fortune. In the prairie, the direction of movement is more or less at the choice of the caravan; among mountains there will often be an alternative, a guess at the most likely pass. But the river with its strong, swift current is the dictator to the raft or to the steamboat. It is a treacherous and capricious dictator. At one season, it may move sluggishly in a channel so narrow that, encountering it for the first time at that point, one can hardly believe that it has travelled already for hundreds of miles, and has yet many hundreds of miles to go; at another season, it may obliterate the low Illinois shore to a horizon of water, while in its bed it runs with a speed such that no man or beast can survive in it. At such times, it carries down human bodies, cattle and houses. At least twice, at St. Louis, the western and the eastern shores have been separated by the fall of bridges, until the designer of the great Eads Bridge devised a structure which could resist the floods. In my own childhood, it was not unusual for the spring freshet to interrupt railway travel; and then the traveller to the East had to take steamboat from the levee up to Alton, at a higher level on the Illinois shore, before he could begin his rail journey. The river is never wholly chartable; it changes its pace, it shifts its channel, unaccountably; it may suddenly efface a sandbar, and throw up another bar where before was navigable water.

It is the River that controls the voyage of Huck and Jim; that will not let them land at Cairo, where Jim could have reached freedom; it is the River that separates them and deposits Huck for a time in the Grangerford household; the River that re-unites them, and then compels upon them the unwelcome company of the King and the Duke. Recurrently we are reminded of its presence and its power.

> When I woke up, I didn't know where I was for a minute. I set up and looked around, a little scared. Then I remembered. The river looked miles and miles across. The moon was so bright I could a counted the drift-logs that went a-slipping along, black and still, hundreds of yards out from shore. Everything was dead quiet, and it looked late, and *smelt* late. You know what I mean—I don't know the words to put it in.
>
> It was kind of solemn, drifting down the big still river, laying on our backs looking up at the stars, and we didn't ever feel like talking loud, and it warn't often that we laughed, only a little kind of a low chuckle. We had mighty good weather as a general thing, and nothing ever happened to us at all, that night, nor the next, nor the next.
>
> Every night we passed towns, some of them away up on black hill-sides, nothing but just a shiny bed of lights, not a house could you see. The fifth night we passed St. Louis, and it was like the whole world lit up. In St. Petersburg they used to say there was twenty or thirty thousand people in St. Louis, but I never believed it till I see that wonderful spread of lights at two o'clock that still night. There warn't a sound there; everybody was asleep.

We come to understand the River by seeing it through the eyes of the Boy; but the Boy is also the spirit of the River. *Huckleberry Finn,* like other great works of imagination, can give to every reader whatever he is capable of taking from it. On the most superficial level of observation, Huck is convincing as a boy. On the same level, the picture of social life on the shores of the Mississippi a hundred years ago is, I feel sure, accurate. On any level, Mark Twain makes you see the River, as it is and was and always will be, more clearly than the author of any other description of a river known to me. But you do not merely see the River, you do not merely become acquainted with it through the senses: you experience the River. Mark Twain, in his later years of success and fame, referred to his early life as a steamboat pilot as the happiest he had known. With all allowance for the illusions of age, we can agree that those years were the years in which he was most fully alive. Certainly, but for his having practised that calling, earned his living by that profession, he would never have gained the understanding which his genius for expression communicates in this book. In the pilot's daily struggle with the River, in the satisfaction of activity, in the constant attention to the River's unpredictable vagaries, his consciousness was fully occupied, and he absorbed knowledge of which, as an artist, he later made use. There are, perhaps, only two ways in which a writer can acquire the understanding of environment which he can later turn to account: by having spent his childhood in that environment—that is, living in it at a period of life in which one experiences much more than one is aware of; and by having had to struggle for a livelihood in that environment—a livelihood bearing no direct relation to any intention of writing about it, of *using* it as literary material. Most of Joseph Conrad's understanding came to him in the latter way. Mark Twain knew the Mississippi in both ways: he had spent his childhood on its banks, and he had earned his living matching his wits against its currents.

Thus the River makes the book a great book. As with Conrad, we are continually reminded of the power and terror of Nature, and the isolation and feebleness of Man. Conrad remains always the European observer of the tropics, the white man's eye contemplating the Congo and its black gods. But Mark Twain is a native, and the River God is his God. It is as a native that he accepts the River God, and it is the subjection of Man that gives to Man his dignity. For without some kind of God, Man is not even very interesting.

Readers sometimes deplore the fact that the story descends to the level of *Tom Sawyer* from the moment that Tom himself reappears. Such readers protest that the escapades invented by Tom, in the attempted "rescue" of Jim, are only a tedious development of themes with which we were already too familiar—even while admitting that the escapades themselves are very amusing, and some of the incidental observations memorable.[1] But it is right that the mood of the end of the book should bring us back to that of the beginning. Or, if this was not the right ending for the book, what ending would have been right?

In *Huckleberry Finn* Mark Twain wrote a much greater book than he could have known he was writing. Perhaps all great works of art mean much more than the author could have been aware of meaning: certainly, *Huckleberry Finn* is the one book of Mark Twain's which, as a whole, has this unconsciousness. So what seems to be the rightness, of reverting at the end of the book to the mood of *Tom Sawyer*, was perhaps unconscious art. For Huckleberry Finn, neither a tragic nor a happy ending would be suitable. No worldly success or social satisfaction, no domestic consummation would be worthy of him; a tragic end also would reduce him to the level of those whom we pity. Huck Finn must come from nowhere and be bound for nowhere. His is not the independence of the typical or symbolic American Pioneer, but the independence of the vagabond. His existence questions the values of America as much as the values of Europe; he is as much an affront to the "pioneer spirit" as he is to "business enterprise"; he is in a state of nature as detached as the state of the saint. In a busy world, he represents the loafer; in an acquisitive and competitive world, he insists on living from hand to mouth. He could not be exhibited in any amorous

[1] *e.g. "Jim* don't know anybody in China."

encounters or engagements, in any of the juvenile affections which are appropriate to Tom Sawyer. He belongs neither to the Sunday School nor to the Reformatory. He has no beginning and no end. Hence, he can only disappear; and his disappearance can only be accomplished by bringing forward another performer to obscure the disappearance in a cloud of whimsicalities.

Like Huckleberry Finn, the River itself has no beginning or end. In its beginning, it is not yet the River; in its end, it is no longer the River. What we call its headwaters is only a selection from among the innumerable sources which flow together to compose it. At what point in its course does the Mississippi become what the Mississippi *means*? It is both one and many; it is the Mississippi of this book only after its union with the Big Muddy— the Missouri; it derives some of its character from the Ohio, the Tennessee and other confluents. And at the end it merely disappears among its deltas: it is no longer there, but it is still where it was, hundreds of miles to the North. The River cannot tolerate any design, to a story which is its story, that might interfere with its dominance. Things must merely happen, here and there, to the people who live along its shores or who commit themselves to its current. And it is as impossible for Huck as for the River to have a beginning or end—a *career*. So the book has the right, the only possible concluding sentence. I do not think that any book ever written ends more certainly with the right words:

> But I reckon I got to light out for the Territory ahead of the rest, because Aunt Sally she's going to adopt me and civilize me, and I can't stand it. I been there before.

The Bostonians
by Henry James, 1886

The New York Edition of James's works, for which he wrote the prefaces now collected in The Art of the Novel, *did not include* The Bostonians. *James later regretted this lost opportunity to introduce and hence make "a much truer and more curious thing" of this novel that was so poorly received in his lifetime. In this introduction to a 1952 edition, Lionel Trilling gives us a critic's perspective on James's "very American tale."*

T*he Bostonians* is one of a pair of
novels, the other being *The Princess Casamassima,* which, in the
family of Henry James's works, have a special connection with each
other, a particular isolate relationship, as of twins. They were
published in the same year, 1886, their previous serial publications
having been in part concurrent, and although *The Bostonians* was
in point of fact the earlier conceived and the first written, they
almost seem to have been composed simultaneously, in a single act
of creation. They are set apart from James's other novels by having
in common a quick responsiveness to the details of the outer world,
an explicit awareness of history and of the movements of society
and civilization, and a curious knowledge of the little groups of
queer people who in small dark rooms agitate the foolish questions
which will eventually be decided on the broad field of the future.
Very likely it was because James was conscious of these qualities
—and, we feel, pleased with them as the evidence of an enlargement
of his social intelligence—that he had especially high hopes that
the two novels would be happily received by the public.

The disappointment of these hopes is well known. With the
exception of his later defeat in the theatre, no check given to James's
ambitions was so disastrous. The English press treated *The Princess*

Casamassima with almost absolute contempt, and if it was more indulgent with *The Bostonians,* this was only because it found satisfaction in a representation of America's queer ways. The American reviewers were outraged by *The Bostonians;* their more lenient response to *The Princess Casamassima* was in part dictated by their settled opinion of the English social system which the book might be thought to satirize. Both novels were called queer and foolish, and their failure caused a serious decline in their author's reputation and market.

When, in April of 1883, James had written out in his notebook the full scenario of *The Bostonians,* he had summarized his intention by saying, "I wished to write a very *American* tale."[1] In this he most notably succeeded. It is possible to say of all James's novels that are set in America—*The Bostonians* is the last until *The Ivory Tower* of some twenty years later—that they have a tone different from that of the novels which are set in Europe. I regard with suspicion my natural impulse to say that this is a specifically "American" tone, for I should not know how to explain with any confidence what that is. Yet it seems to me worth observing that, as against the heavy chiaroscuro which in *The Princess Casamassima* is appropriate to the rich, clotted past of civilization which that novel evokes, *The Bostonians* seems suffused with the "dry American light," and that it is marked by a comicality which has rather more kinship with American humour than with British humour, or with wit of any transatlantic kind. "She was heroic, she was sublime, the whole moral history of Boston was reflected in her displaced spectacles"; "It is true that if she had been a boy, she would have borne some relation to a girl"; " 'She was determined she wouldn't be a patient,

---

[1]The tense of this cannot pass without notice. James was not to write the book until two years later, yet, like Menander, when once he had completed the scenario, he felt that the main work was behind him, so natural to him was the act of writing, so little uncertainty intervened for him between the intention and the act. Yet no reader of the notebooks can but feel how much was conceived in the writing that could never have been conceived in the scenario, however "divine" James thought the "principle of the scenario" to be.

and it seemed as if the only way not to be one was to be a doctor' "—humour is latent in all of James's writing, but I can bring to mind no other of his novels in which it breaks out of latency into the memorable free overtness of such sentences as these and of scenes analogous to these sentences.

And as a representation of the American actuality, *The Bostonians* is in every way remarkable, the more so because it is so original. James's Boston, Cambridge, and Cape Cod are superbly rendered, and these localities may still be known—for they have changed less than most American places—through his descriptions of them. No American writer before James had so fully realized the contemporary American scene of moral action and social existence. Nor had the nature of the American social existence itself ever been so brilliantly suggested. Manners have changed since James wrote, but not the peculiar tenuity of the fabric of American social life. The London of *The Princess Casamassima* is no doubt the city of dreadful loneliness, and the barriers of class which it represents are real enough, yet the story sees to it that people at social poles from each other shall meet and become involved with each other. It is thus perfectly in the tradition of the English novel, which characteristically likes the social mixture to be thick and variously composed, and this is a literary preference which corresponds, at whatever distance, to an actuality of English life. But in the America of *The Bostonians,* as in the America that Tocqueville had observed some fifty years before, society is but little organized to allow for variety and complexity and the social atoms seem to have a centrifugal tendency. Basil Ransom lives in New York with no other companion than his little variety actress. He makes every effort to avoid the company of his cousin, Mrs. Luna, and she, a lady of family and means, seems to have no social circle at all. It is of the essence of Olive Chancellor's nature that she cannot endure social intercourse; a speech to a crowd is her notion of human communication, and she cannot laugh. Verena Tarrant has presumably never had a friend until Olive Chancellor institutes their ambiguous alliance. Dr. Prance lives in virtual solitude. Miss Birdseye, having devoted a long life to humanity, becomes herself an object of devotion, but rather as if she were an old school, or a dear, outworn ideal.[2]

The notion of Henry James as a political novelist usually evokes surprise, even amusement. And yet politics—at least of the sort to which he devoted his attention in *The Bostonians* and *The Princess Casamassima*—may be thought of as but a more than usually explicit instance of the kind of consideration with which James habitually dealt. For perhaps the trait which is most definitive of James's temper of mind is the dialectical nature of his thought. Virtually all of his fiction is composed out of the setting against each other of two great elemental principles of life. These two principles are constant, although circumstance changes their appearance and their relative value. They may be thought of as energy and inertia; or spirit and matter; or spirit and letter; or force and form; or radicalism and conservatism; or creation and possession; or Libido and Thanatos. In the simpler manifestations of the dialectic, the first term of the grandiose duality is generally regarded with unalloyed sympathy and identified with the ideality of youth, or art, or truth, or America; the second term is regarded with hostility and held to be one with age, or convention, or philistinism, or Europe. But the dialectic is not allowed to remain simple for very long. Daisy Miller's crude, innocent defiance of European conventions is as right as rain, but *Madame de Mauves* suggests that only a small change in circumstance can make American innocence a downright malevolence. Art as against the philistine morality may not always have the right of things, for creation may corrupt itself into its opposite, possession, as in *The Author of Beltraffio*. Life may be seen to express itself in death, and through death. And in *The Birthplace* James

---

[2]The character of Miss Birdseye scandalized Boston because it was thought to be a portrait of Elizabeth Peabody, Hawthorne's famous reforming sister-in-law. Beyond "invasion of privacy," it is hard to understand what the ground of offence was supposed to be, for if Miss Birdseye is indeed a portrait, it is the tenderest and most endearing imaginable. William James—who had a poor opinion of *The Bostonians* in any case—undertook to rebuke his brother for his failure of taste, and Henry replied in a letter which has become the classic statement of the relation of the novelist's imagination to real persons.

seems to be saying that the truth can exist only in and through the life of institutions.

The nature of the terms of James's dialectic suggests why his fiction is always momentous. And a mind whose indigenous form of thought is dialectical will naturally be attracted by and at ease with the momentous opposing terms of politics. It is not only when his subject is avowedly political that James is aware of a threatened imbalance of the right order of life; with him, as with Shakespeare, the possibility of the triumph of anarchy and chaos is an omnipresent and defining element of his thought.

A comparison of the contemporary movements on which James's two political novels base themselves may at first seem to give all the advantage to that of *The Princess Casamassima*. In a struggle for general social justice there is a natural weightiness and dignity, and in a violent revolutionary intention there is an immediate possibility of tragic drama. But the doctrinaire demand for an equality of the sexes seems to promise but a wry and constricted tale, unless it be treated, as Aristophanes treated it in the classic instances of *Lysistrata* and *The Thesmophoriazusæ*, as frankly comic, and as affirming rather than denying the erotic community between men and women. The movement of female emancipation, which became endemic in America and in the Protestant countries of Europe in the nineteenth century, was almost exclusively social and legal in its programme and even had, although not always, an outright antierotic bias which exposed it to the imputation of being without dignity and merely crankish.

But exactly in seizing on the qualities of the woman's rights agitation which were in themselves the least profound and the most a perversion of essential humanity, James possessed himself of a subject that was of even larger significance than that of the revolutionary Anarchism of *The Princess Casamassima*. A movement of social revolution may or may not question the culture in which it exists, and it is possible to say of social revolutions that they do not in fact question cultures as much as they seem to and say they do. But a movement of sexual revolution is to be understood as a question which a culture puts to itself, and down to its very roots.

It is a question about what it means to be a man and what it means to be a woman—about the quality of being which people wish to have. James was interested in the thin vagaries of a female movement of reform only as they suggested a conflict between men and women that went far deeper than any quarrel over rights and equalities. This antagonism was certainly not the formal, chivalrous battle of marching and counter-marching and "Gentlemen of France, you may fire first!" which Meredith and Shaw delighted in—it was the bitter total war which Strindberg perceived and which found its fullest ideological and artistic expression in the work of D. H. Lawrence.

Tocqueville, whose great book, James tells us, was a favourite of the hero of *The Bostonians*, had noted the beginnings of sexual disorientation in America; and in James's own time, American observers who were not bound by convention, men so unlike as Walt Whitman and Henry Adams, were aware that something had gone wrong with the sexual life of the nation. Adams spoke of American men as having abandoned their sexuality for business and the machine, and as having induced in American women an indifference to maternity. And James, when he had set down his intention of "writing a very *American* tale," went on to say, "I asked myself what was the most salient and peculiar point of our social life. The answer was: the situation of women, the decline of the sentiment of sex. . . ."

No more than Tocqueville or Henry Adams or D. H. Lawrence did James understand the sexual situation as an isolated fact, however momentous. For him, as for them, it was the sign of a general diversion of the culture from the course of nature. This he makes plain by his choice of a hero for *The Bostonians*. By choosing a Southerner—rather than the Westerner he had first thought of— James gained an immediate and immeasurable advantage, by one stroke setting his story beyond the danger of seeming to be a mere law-bicker between men and women. By involving the sexual conflict with even a late adumbration of the immense, tragic struggle between North and South, he made it plain that his story had to do with a cultural crisis. Nor could this crisis seem merely local, for North and South, as James understands them, represent the opposing elements in that elaborate politics of culture which has been the great essential subject of the literature of the nineteenth and twentieth centuries.

The South had never had a vigorous intellectual life, and of the systematic apologists for its customs and manners as against those of an ever more powerful industrial capitalism, only a very few had been men of real intellectual authority. Yet with the strange previsionary courage which led him, in *The Princess Casamassima*, to imagine types of political character unknown to his own time but familiar to ours, James conceived Basil Ransom as if he were the leading, ideal intelligence of the group of gifted men who, a half-century later, were to rise in the South and to muster in its defence all the force of intelligent romantic conservatism. Rejecting impatiently the sentimental legend of the South, admitting the Southern faults and falsities the more easily because they believed that no civilization can be anything but imperfect, they yet said that the South stood for a kind of realism which the North, with its abstract intellectuality, was forgetting to its cost. Like their proto-martyr Ransom, they asserted a distrust of theory, an attachment to tradition, and, above all, the tragic awareness of the intractability of the human circumstance.

But Basil Ransom is more daring than any of his intellectual descendants of the South. He has the courage of the collateral British line of romantic conservatives—he is akin to Yeats, Lawrence, and Eliot in that he experiences his cultural fears in the most personal way possible, translating them into sexual fear, the apprehension of the loss of manhood. "The whole generation is womanised," he says, "the masculine tone is passing out of the world; it's a feminine, a nervous, hysterical, chattering, canting age, an age of hollow phrases and false delicacy and exaggerated solicitudes and coddled sensibilities, which, if we don't soon look out, will usher in the reign of mediocrity, of the feeblest and flattest and the most pretentious that has ever been. The masculine character, the ability to dare and endure, to know and yet not fear reality, to look the world in the face and take it for what it is—a very queer and partly very base mixture—that is what I want to preserve, or rather, as I may say, to recover; and I must say that I don't in the least care what becomes of you ladies while I make the attempt."

And the fear of the loss of manhood, which we are familiar with in Yeats, in Lawrence, and in *The Waste Land,* is given reason for its existence everywhere in *The Bostonians.* The book is full of malign, archaic influences. It is not for nothing that Olive Chancellor's sister is named Mrs. Luna—with her shallow, possessive sexuality she might as well have been named Mrs. Hecate. The very name of Olive Chancellor might suggest a deteriorated Minerva, presiding in homosexual chastity over the Athens of the New World. The meeting of Olive's colleagues is referred to as a rendezvous of witches on the Brocken, a characterization which is supported throughout the book by James's rather unpleasant sense of the threatening sordidness of all women except those in their first youth. Verena is conceived as a sort of Iphigenia in Tauris, forced to preside as the priestess of the sacrifice of humanity. Basil Ransom is explicit in his feeling that when he is with Olive Chancellor he is not "safe." And indeed his position is at all times a precarious one. We have the impression that he is the only man in Boston, among hordes of doctrinaire Bacchæ, and certainly he is the only man in the book—Verena's poor suitor, Burrage, lives under the shadow of his mother; Dr. Tarrant is a kind of shaman, gloomily doing sexual service of some dim, grim kind to deprived Boston ladies; and Matthias Pardon, the newspaper man, is the castrate priest of the huge idol of publicity, which, in the dialectic of the book, stands in hateful opposition to the life of emotion and true sexuality. Perhaps the novel's crucial scene is that which takes place in Memorial Hall at Harvard, when Ransom must insist to Verena on the tragic fate of the young men who had died in the recent war. These had been his enemies, but the danger of battle had never been so great as the sexual danger of his present civil situation.

There is one biographical circumstance of *The Bostonians* which ought to be mentioned in any account of the novel. I have no doubt that it bears in an important way upon the personal problems of Henry James's own life which are, we must inevitably suppose, implied by Ransom's fears. But the investigation of these problems lies outside my competence and my purpose, and I mention the circumstance only for reasons that are purely literary, only because, that is, awareness of it is likely to make for a warmer understanding of the book.

In 1881 James visited his country and his family for the first time since 1876, when he had made his decision to establish his home in England. From the first the visit was not a happy one. James disliked Boston, where he stayed to be near his parents in Cambridge, and he was bored and restless. In January he went to stay with Henry Adams in Washington and there, on the 30th of the month, he received the telegram announcing his mother's serious illness which was intended to prepare him for her death. It was James's first familial loss and it shocked and saddened him deeply, yet it also, as he writes of it in his notebook, moved him to a kind of joy. He had always known that he loved his mother, but not until he saw her in her shroud did he know how tender his love was. Mrs. James had been a quiet woman, with none of the spirited quality of her husband, the elder Henry James. But her son wrote of her, "She was our life, she was the house, she was the keystone of the arch. She held us all together, and without her we are scattered reeds. She was patience, she was wisdom, she was exquisite maternity." And as his impassioned memorial of her draws to its close, he says: "It was a perfect mother's life—the life of a perfect wife. To bring her children into the world—to expend herself, for years, for their happiness and welfare—then, when they had reached a full maturity and were absorbed in the world and their own interests—to lay herself down in her ebbing strength and yield up her pure soul to the celestial power that had given her this divine commission."

James stayed with his father and his sister Alice until May, when, at his father's insistence, he returned to England and work. But in December the news came of his father's imminent death. The elder Henry James, it was said, had no wish to survive his wife; in his last illness he refused food and gently faded away. The younger Henry arrived too late to see his father for the last time, too late even for the funeral. William James's famous letter of farewell to their "sacred old Father" also arrived too late, but Henry took it to the grave in the Cambridge cemetery and read it aloud, sure, as he wrote to William, that the father "heard somewhere out of the depths of the still bright winter air."

His mother was the strength that is not power as the world knows power, the strength of conservation, the unseen, unregarded, seemingly unexerted force that holds things to their centre; she had lived the ancient elemental course of life, which is without theory or formulation, too certain of itself and too much at one with itself even to aspire. His father, according to his peculiar lights, had had "the ability to dare and endure, to know and yet not to fear reality." And during his sad visit to his parental land in 1883, the last for twenty years, when the parental family had come to an end, Henry James wrote out the scenario of *The Bostonians*, which is a story of the parental house divided against itself, of the keystone falling from the arch, of the sacred mothers refusing their commission and the sacred fathers endangered.

V. S. PRITCHETT ON

The Red Badge of Courage
by Stephen Crane, 1895

H. G. Wells's idea that "Crane's writing suggests Whistler rather than Tolstoy" is the point of departure for this introduction in which British author and critic V. S. Pritchett examines the distinctly American character of The Red Badge of Courage.

Stephen Crane is one of those writers who, after one startling *tour de force,* burn themselves out. American journalism seized him, labelled him, thrust him into "real life" as a war correspondent and annulled his imaginative talent and health. At twenty-eight he was dead. Fittingly he has become a legend, a symbol of the misused artist. It is natural to compare Crane with his Scottish contemporary Stevenson, even though Crane disliked the comparison. The two looked astonishingly alike; they shocked and they charmed. Crane's Methodist background is matched by Stevenson's Calvinist upbringing and both men, we notice, moved to an ironical, unbelieving, moral dandyism which affected their prose. They believe in the word and not the Word and are constantly surprising us with phrases that come to an ear trained by the pulpit and the Bible. (In *The Red Badge of Courage,* Crane will refer to "the remonstrance of the guns.") Crane is a very literary writer and he was compared, as he complained, to everyone from Tolstoy to Loti and Conrad. We get near his essence in H. G. Wells's remark that Crane's writing suggested Whistler rather than Tolstoy; Wells is the only European critic to have kept in mind the distinguishing American character of Crane's work.

The fact is that Crane was as profoundly American in his disposition for writing fable or poetic romance, as were Hawthorne, Poe, Melville, and Henry James. *The Red Badge of Courage* is not simply one of the earliest realistic novels about war written in Tolstoy's sceptical and anti-romantic spirit; it is a poetic fable about the attempt of a young man to discover a real identity in battle. The case becomes stranger when we remember that Crane wrote this book before he had had any real experience of war at all. (It was only after writing *The Red Badge of Courage* that he became a war correspondent.) A study of Tolstoy and a number of Memoirs of the American Civil War were his principal guides for a book that is a distillation for special ends; we are not told where the battle is, for what reasons, or, indeed, what the military situation is. In other novelists who write about war, from Vigny to Tolstoy, from Tolstoy to Hemingway and Jules Romains, we *know* because they immerse us in what they lived. Crane, by an astonishing bound of imagination, has created battle as the simple and confused soldier sees it, but for reasons that are psychological, i.e. he is describing an interior battle, a battle of the spirit. The battle itself is compared at times with a mad religion, a sectarian conflict. The story might well be an artist's transposition of a dilemma of religious conscience; has been romantically committed to "fight the good fight," is frightened into running away, and then has to reassemble his self-respect out of fear, doubt, and lies and learn how to live with his experience. It is quite true that all Crane's stories are concerned with fear, but with fear as a moral ferment, fear as the question put to the American dream of toughness, the emotion natural to the lonely uncertainty about who or what one is. The desire of all the Crane heroes is to find an identity by belonging to something. The theme is at the heart of *Maggie,* in the early Bowery Tales; in *The Red Badge of Courage,* and even in short, half-comic stories like *The Bride Comes to Yellow Sky, The Blue Hotel,* and the dramatic report of *The Open Boat.*

In his psychological observation and in his ear for speech Crane is one of the founders of American realism as we have known it since his time. In him it moves towards the fabulous and poetic;

occasionally it sprawls and becomes rhetorical—see the end of *Maggie*. He appears to have been bedevilled by the theory that a writer must know from personal experience the thing he is writing about—a theory he certainly did not stick to in *The Red Badge of Courage* except in an esoteric sense, and did stick to in *The Open Boat* and his war reporting. The feeling for "life" is related to anxiety about toughness and to the American approval of aggressiveness and to fighting as an initiation rite. Here is an excellent portrait of a barman from the Bowery:

> He sat on a table in the Johnson home, and dangled his check legs with an enticing nonchalance. His hair was curled down over his forehead in an oiled bang. His pugged nose seemed to revolt from contact with a bristling moustache of short, wire-like hairs. His blue double-breasted coat, edged with black braid, was buttoned close to a red puff tie, and his patent leather shoes looked like weapons. His mannerisms stamped him as a man who had a correct sense of his personal superiority. There was valour and contempt for circumstances in the glance of his eye.

Shoes like weapons! Crane's feeling for fighting, temper, rage, and pride is innate. (He said he learned about battle on the football field.) Sticks, stones, rifles, artillery, dray horses—and once—a fire engine bashing its way along, became valued symbols. In the Bowery Tales the fighting, drunken slum characters occasionally suspect that there is something else in life besides brawling but they are not quite sure what it is. When Maggie's drunken mother becomes morally indignant at her fate and maudlin about her death, a dim, perverse light has been lit. Crane always sharpened the irony of his writing and rigorously censored what there was in him of the didactic. He is not cynical but his view of life is a hard one: we must fight to live but we shall get nothing out of it. We live and die alone. No one will ever know the secrets that both shame us and keep us going. Maggie is alone, the absurd Swede in *The Blue Hotel* is alone on his fatal see-saw of fear and bravado, the anonymous young man in *The Red Badge of Courage* is alone.

Crane was a brilliant impressionist and has strong affinities with the Impressionist painters. As they sought to record infinitesimal particles of light, he sought to record the innumerable glints of significant natural and psychological detail in the prolonged battle scene of *The Red Badge of Courage*. It is a search sustained by a poetic fervour which usually subsides before it becomes rhetoric, and then rises again with a sea-like motion as it meets the next incident. He is always simple and explicit, alert for the random irony. He is aware of the ironical disparity between what imagination and tradition suggest and what in fact is seen. Jim Conklin, dying of his wounds, walks with his court of mourners like a spectre seeking a place to die. When he does fall down to die, Crane will notice that his left shoulder hits the ground first and that he gives "a little commonplace smile." The death of Conklin is tragic; but it is horrible, too, because in its final agonies it is grotesque. So grotesque that another dying soldier starts boasting that he himself will not die with such a lack of dignity. Death exposes; it is the final betrayal in lives which—one now sees—have been most mercifully protected by shames, concealments, and lies:

> The youth could see that the soles of his shoes had been worn to the thinness of writing paper and from a great rent in one of them the dead foot projected piteously. And it was as if fate had betrayed the soldier. In death it exposed to his enemies that poverty which in life he had perhaps concealed from his friends.

The irony is relentless; the red badge of courage itself is a soldier's wound and the young man does indeed win it. But it is false. For the boy gained his badge when, in a panic, he struggled with one of his own panic-stricken fellows and was clubbed by him. Crane, the lapsed Methodist, could not have been more thoroughly lost to his faith; and one can see in this poem, if one cares to do so, that he is outside, reduced to man's primitive state, in the older, madder religion of war.

With his gift for metaphor—a gift which is not without its affectations—Crane once described a woman going in black to a prayer meeting "like a limited funeral." When we sit back and reflect on the importance of *The Red Badge of Courage*, this phrase comes to mind. The tale *is* a *tour de force*, but it is a minor work. As a novel about war it is itself a "limited funeral." If we compare his work with Tolstoy's—which was his direct inspiration—we see that Tolstoy's reflections on war and his war narratives are not derived at second hand from literature in order to enact a drama of personal salvation; they are the work of a man who had been a soldier and one who has the sense of campaign and of the complete military life. Wars do not occur for the purpose of providing private moral tests. We would not gather from Crane's little masterpiece that he was describing a battle in a civil war—the most dreadful of all wars, but sometimes called the purest—where large, public moral issues profoundly affecting the growth and spirit of a nation were being decided. The war appears to be meaningless. We have no strong impression that the soldiers he describes are really civilians. The result is that the tale has length, very much in the manner of picaresque writing, but no depth—or at any rate no more than a bias towards privacy. His tale is a marvellous one for a very young man to have constructed out of nothing, but it remains a brilliant collection of impressions and surfaces. Perhaps he felt a romantic guilt in not having known the real thing, a guilt not uncommon among post-war generations. Romantic, restless, dipping into "life" all over the world, a journalist-*voyeur* with his own Hamlet-like train of guilts and scruples, killing a frail body in the search for a physical justification, Crane is a writer who is arrested at the stage of personality. Achieving it, his talent declined. We might now be saying his life as a writer was tragic, had he lived out the normal span.

The House of Mirth
by Edith Wharton, 1905

Edith Wharton's House of Mirth *was an immediate best seller in 1905, and in the view of critic and social historian Irving Howe, one of her most powerful novels. In his sympathetic introduction, he describes the moral vision and technical mastery that give permanent distinction to her portrait of the American aristocracy at the turn of the century.*

The name of Edith Wharton still appears with some prominence in histories of American writing, and most literate people know one or two of her books, usually *Ethan Frome* or *The Age of Innocence;* but it would be a mistake to conclude that she is one of those writers whose work is currently felt to be alive, forming a notable pressure on the minds of cultivated readers. She has not been subject to the mixed blessing of a literary revival, as have Henry James and F. Scott Fitzgerald. Contemporary writers seldom regard her as a guiding influence or ancestor. Some of her best books, *The Reef* and *Summer,* are out of print. And the general feeling seems to be that she has been quietly tucked away in the literary past, safely consigned to the dust of academic consideration.

This is a pity, since at her best Mrs. Wharton is a writer of force and distinction. Why she has suffered neglect, however, is not difficult to surmise. Mrs. Wharton is a most uneven novelist, first-rate in a few books and dismal in a good many more, and there still lingers the painful impression created by the popular fiction she turned out during the later years of her life. As she grew older, her social conservatism and literary traditionalism tended to become stiff and querulous, so that she found herself cast in an unprofitable conflict with the younger writers. (To Sinclair Lewis she wrote a trifle wistfully in 1921: "I had long since resigned myself to the idea that I was regarded by you all as the—say the Mrs. Humphry Ward of the Western Hemisphere.") Her books were too easy to "place" historically, and thereby to dismiss as reflections of the rise and fall of the New York commercial aristocracy which had come into its wealth during the mid-nineteenth century, for it was assumed that the fate of her class would be the fate of her work. Also, she has not been very fortunate in her critics, most of whom have treated her novels in terms too narrowly sociological. They have failed to see or honor what was most impressive in them: an exacting standard of technical performance, a moral vision both intense and grave, and a revealed spirit so troubled and austere as to leave upon each line she wrote an unmistakable, an utterly personal signature.

I

One of Mrs. Wharton's novels that most deserves to be honored is *The House of Mirth*, published in 1905 and her first major piece of work. She had written books before then, such as her collection of stories, *The Greater Inclination*, which appeared in 1899, and her somewhat stuffy historical novel, *The Valley of Decision*, which came out in 1902. But it is with *The House of Mirth*, her most powerful if not her most polished novel, that she begins her career as a portraitist of the upper segments of American society.

Mrs. Wharton was one of the two or three American writers to know fully and from the inside what the life of the rich in this country is really like. Henry James had used that life as an occasion for fables of freedom and circumstance in his later books; F. Scott Fitzgerald, an interloper in the world of wealth, was to collect brilliant guesses and fragments of envious insight; John O'Hara has felt his way along the provincial outposts of the America that made its money fast and late. But no American writer has known quite so deeply as Mrs. Wharton what it means, both as privilege and burden, to grow up in a family of the established rich: a family where there was enough money and had been money long enough for talk about it to seem vulgar, and where conspicuous effort to make more of it seemed more vulgar. While a final literary estimate of her novels can hardly be determined by such considerations, one reason for continuing to value novels like *The House of Mirth, The Custom of the Country,* and *The Age of Innocence* is the shrewdness with which Mrs. Wharton, through an expert scrutiny of manners, is able to discriminate among the gradations of power and status in the world of the rich. To read these books is to discover how the novel of manners can register both the surface of social life and the inner vibrations of spirit that surface reveals, suppresses, and distorts.

Mrs. Wharton was born Edith Newbold Jones in 1862. Her family had made their money in merchant shipping and had settled into the narrow, upright mode of life enjoyed by a wealthy class not yet threatened by the clamor and competition of the *nouveaux riches.* Tepid in spirit, sedate in tone, and conservative in morality, this class forms in Mrs. Wharton's novels the touchstone for a range of social contrasts as well as the object of some of her most stringent criticism. It was a class that believed in good manners, good English, good form. It believed in culture, but as a static and finished quantity: a culture epitomized in rows of books by standard authors in dark libraries. In her girlhood Edith Jones received all the advantages that growing up in such an environment tends to produce. She was carefully educated; she was taken on those ceremonial tours of Europe which formed so enviable a part in the life of wealthy Americans during the nineteenth century; she inherited a number of fixed moral premises which later she could neither dispose of nor live with; she read the great poets and historians with a reverence that was never to fade. Edith Jones was a serious girl, perhaps even a solemn one, and she began to write poetry, some of which at the recommendation of Longfellow first appeared in 1880 in the *Atlantic Monthly.*

Toward the world in which she grew up, Mrs. Wharton retained a mixture of feelings that anticipates, in a curious way, the attitudes later American writers would have to their immigrant childhood and youth. It was all too fatally *her* world, beyond choice or escape, and it would serve her as lifelong memory, lifelong subject, perhaps lifelong trauma. It was a world dissolving before her eyes and from book to book she charted the phases of its dissolution, half in the cool spirit of the anthropologist, half with an intensely personal regret. The novelist Louis Auchincloss has provided an excellent description of Mrs. Wharton and her milieu:

> The thing that was going on in Mrs. Wharton's New York of this period, and which she chose as the subject of her main study, was the assault upon an old and conservative group by the multitudes enriched, and fabulously enriched, by the business expansion of the preceding decades. The New York of the pre-assault era was the New York that she was later and nostalgically to describe in *The Age of Innocence,* the town of sober brownstone houses with high stoops, of an Academy of Music with shabby red and gold boxes, of long midday lunches with madeira, of husbands who never went "downtown," of a sense of precedence that was military in its strictness. . . . It was a city that was worldly beyond a doubt, but worldly with a sense of order and form, with plenty of leisure time in which art, music and literature could play a moderated role. The people from this world may lack strength of character but their inertia is coupled with taste. . . .

That Mrs. Wharton loved this New York is perfectly clear, yet it also left her dissatisfied, on edge, unfulfilled. She yearned for a way of life conducive to greater intellectual risks and yielding greater emotional rewards than her friends and family could imagine, and only after a time did she find it in her dedication to writing.

At the age of twenty-three she married Edward Wharton, a wealthy young man quite devoid of intellectual interests, with whom for a good many years she tried to build a common life through sociability and travel. The effort was a failure. One gains the sense of a young woman struggling desperately with her boredom, her belief in propriety, her imperious responsibility, and her unreleased energies. Repression formed a major if unacknowledged theme in her novels and stories, repression that she portrayed with such a grim, almost voracious fatalism and that seems forever to be closing in upon her characters as if to cheat them of the love and pleasure they desire. During the years of her unhappy marriage, as well as the long gray years of her separation from Wharton, his mental illness and their divorce—even, it would seem, during the time of her friendship with Walter Berry, the cultivated American lawyer who was the great love of her life—there must always have been present to Mrs. Wharton an acute sense of the power and the cost of repression. Henry James, her good friend and occasional literary influence, was a writer for whom heroism was sometimes not to be distinguished from renunciation; but for Mrs. Wharton heroism was often not to be distinguished from mere self-denial.

As Mrs. Wharton traced the defeat of her heroines she depicted repression as the dismal price we pay for living in an organized society. She also felt an exile at the very center of her clan; a current of estrangement worked its way through her books, for which one explanation, admittedly speculative, has been offered by the distinguished critic Edmund Wilson:

> It has been asserted by persons who should be in a position to know that Edith Wharton had some reason for believing herself to have been an illegitimate child and that her family rather let her down from the point of view of social backing—which would account for the curiously perfunctory, idyllic and unreal way in which she writes of her parents in *A Backward Glance* [Mrs. Wharton's autobiography], as contrasted with her bitter picture, in her novels of old New York, of the cruelty of social convention and the tyranny of the family group, as well as for her preoccupation with the miseries of extra-marital love affairs and the problems of young women who have to think about marrying for money and position.

How much weight to give to Wilson's remark about Mrs. Wharton's childhood we do not know, and probably will not until her papers at Yale University Library are opened in 1968. Considering her extreme reticence in personal matters, we may not know even then. Nor does it matter very much, because the themes Wilson observes in her work, whether or not they can be traced directly to her personal experience, are important and recurrent. And their presence strengthens one's impression that for Mrs. Wharton the act of becoming a writer meant not merely a choice of vocation but a kind of saving therapy, a personal liberation.

Soon after the appearance of *The House of Mirth* Mrs. Wharton took her place as a notable figure in American literary life, and from then until her death in 1937, by which time her reputation had sharply declined, she produced an enormous amount of fiction. She published fourteen novels, nine novelettes, eleven volumes of stories and several books of criticism, travel description and autobiography. For even the most professional of writers, this would constitute an imposing output, but for a woman who issued her first important novel after the age of forty and as a rule worked only in the morning so as to leave the rest of her day free for social duties, it is astonishing.

Quite as astonishing and far more important is the range of her writing. There cannot be much dispute as to which are her best books: *The House of Mirth, The Reef, The Custom of the Country, Ethan Frome, Summer, The Age of Innocence,* and a selection that could be made from her short stories. In *The House of Mirth* Mrs. Wharton approached the heavy atmosphere of fatality we associate with naturalism; in *The Reef* she composed a delicate study of personal relationships; in *The Custom of the Country* she turned to abrasive satire, anticipating the best of Sinclair Lewis. But she could also write about the poor and neglected and write about them with a firm, uncondescending sympathy. *Ethan Frome* is a bitter New England tragedy; *Summer,* a harsh account of backcountry New England; "The Bunner Sisters," a realistic novelette about the miseries of two poor women in New York. Perhaps Mrs. Wharton's most finished work is *The Age of Innocence,* a suave mixture of satire and nostalgia, which portrays the social and pictorial background of old New York.

Not even her warmest champions are likely to claim that Edith Wharton was a great writer. But it is worth remarking that even while she clung to her conservative views about the techniques of fiction and resisted the literary experimentalism of the twentieth century, Mrs. Wharton employed the novel with a greater capacity for realizing its range of thematic and tonal possibilities than most other American writers. The complexity of her achievement has still to be acknowledged, and her day of recognition still to come.

II

The House of Mirth begins in a manner characteristic of Mrs. Wharton, with a forthright attack on her material, hard and direct, and without expository preparation. The elaborate hovering over the imagined scene so habitual to Henry James, a novelist with whom Mrs. Wharton has been linked too easily, is not at all her way of doing things, for she is a blunt and often impatient writer. "My last page," she once said, "is always latent in my first," and at least in *The House of Mirth* the claim is true. At the very outset Mrs. Wharton groups the main figures of her story—Lily Bart, Lawrence Selden, Sim Rosedale—in several vignettes of typical conduct. These comprise not so much a full novelistic scene as a succession of compressed, scenic fragments, each juxtaposed so as to yield quick information and stir immediate concern. "The art of rendering life in fiction," Mrs. Wharton wrote, "can never . . . be anything . . . but the disengaging of crucial moments from the welter of experience."

That is precisely what she does in the opening chapters. Lily is first seen through the eyes of Selden, the cultivated lawyer who is to serve as a standard of moral refinement and an instance of personal inadequacy. "Her discretions," writes Mrs. Wharton in one of those bristling sentences that do their necessary damage to both Lily and Selden, "interested him almost as much as her imprudences: he was so sure that both were part of the same carefully-elaborated plan." Shrewd yet not sufficiently daring, Selden here begins to enact that rhythm of involvement and withdrawal, advance and retreat, which will mark his relations with Lily until the very end of the book. He entices her with a vision of a life better than the one she has chosen, yet fails to give her the unquestioning masculine support which might enable her to live by that vision.

We see Lily and Selden together, each a little uneasy with the other, yet decidedly attractive as a pair and civilized enough to take pleasure in knowing they are attractive—Mrs. Wharton had a fine eye for the pictorial arrangements in the social intercourse between the sexes. They amuse and test each other with small talk—Mrs. Wharton had a fine ear for the conversation that carries subtle burdens of meaning. We see Lily and Selden taking each other's measure, Lily admiring his quiet style yet aware of his handicaps and hesitations, Selden admiring her beauty yet aware that "she was so evidently the victim of the civilization which had produced her, that the links of her bracelet seemed like manacles chaining her to her fate." This striking sentence is put to several uses: it prepares us for the ordeal of a Lily Bart neither at ease with nor in rebellion against her life as a dependent of the rich; it provides a convincing example of Selden's gift for superior observation; and because ironically, this gift is matched with his tendency to self-protection and self-justification, it suggests that Mrs. Wharton will not require or allow Selden to serve as a voice of final judgment in the novel. Given the caustic style of these opening pages, we are entitled to suppose that Mrs. Wharton will reserve that task for herself.

There quickly follows the encounter between Lily and Rosedale. At this point Rosedale is mostly stock caricature, the "pushy little Jew" taken from the imagery of social, that is, polite, anti-Semitism; later Mrs. Wharton will do more with him. Rosedale trips Lily in a lie and is not gentleman enough to refrain from stressing his petty triumph, but the main point is that Lily, usually so nimble at handling social difficulties, has been caught off balance because she is still glowing with the pleasure of having met Selden. This too prefigures a major theme: the price, here in embarrassment and later in deprivation, that genuine emotion exacts from those who have chosen a life of steady calculation. Coming always at inconvenient moments—for it is Selden's presence which repeatedly causes her to falter—the spontaneous feelings Lily neither can nor wishes to suppress will lead to her social undoing.

Lovely as Lily Bart seems, Mrs. Wharton is careful to establish a firm dissociation between author and heroine, though never to the point of withdrawing her compassion. The similarity between Rosedale and Lily, each trying in a particular way to secure a foothold in the world of the rich, is faintly suggested by Mrs. Wharton as a cue for later elaboration. She also introduces the figure of Lily's cousin, Jack Stepney, who serves as Lily's Smerdyakov, the "double" grossly reflecting and disfiguring her ambitions. Lily, as Mrs. Wharton dryly remarks, "understood his motives, for her own course was guided by as nice calculations."

And then, to climax these introductory chapters, there come two moments of symbolic action, each isolating the central role of money in the life of Lily Bart. The first is Balzacian: Judy Trenor, the rich hostess and for a time Lily's friend, "who could have afforded to lose a thousand a night [at cards], had left the table clutching such a heap of bills that she had been unable to shake hands with her guests when they bade her good night." The second is probably beyond Balzac: Lily, having lost too much money at cards, retires to her room in the Trenor house and notices "two little lines near her mouth, faint flaws in the smooth curve of her cheek." Frightened, she thinks they may be caused by the electric light. She turns it off, leaving only the candles on her dressing-table. "The white oval of her face swam out waveringly from a background of shadows, the uncertain light blurring it like a haze; but the two lines about the mouth remained."

The House of Mirth rests on the assumption that moral values can be tested in a novel by dramatizing the relationships between fixed social groups and mobile characters. In the friction thus engendered, moral values come to be seen not as abstract categories to be imposed upon human experience but as problems, elements in the effort of men to cope with conflicting desires and obligations. At every point Lily's history is defined by her journey from one social group to another, a journey both she and her friends regard as a fall, a catastrophe. Only dimly, and then after much pain and confusion, does she realize that this social fall may have positive moral consequences. For us, who have followed her story with that mixture of ironic detachment and helpless compassion Mrs. Wharton trains us to feel, it should be clear all the while that the meanings of the book emerge through a series of contrasts between a fixed scale of social place and an evolving measure of moral value.

It is as if the world within which Lily moves consists of a series of descending planes, somewhat like a modern stage, and each part of the novel is devoted to showing the apparent success with which Lily survives one drop after another but also how each apparent success bears within itself the impetus toward still another fall. As

Mrs. Wharton remarks: "If [Lily] slipped she recovered her footing, and it was only afterward that she was aware of having recovered it each time on a slightly lower level." There is, to be sure, much more to *The House of Mirth* than these expert notations of social status. There is a portrait of a young woman trapped in her confusions of value, a story of love destroyed through these confusions, and a harsh enactment of Mrs. Wharton's sentiments about human loss and doom. But all of these take on their particular cogency, their fictional shape, under the pressures of the social milieu evoked in the novel.

Mrs. Wharton's great theme—the dispossession of the old New York aristocracy by the vulgar new rich—is not quite as visible in *The House of Mirth* as in *The Custom of the Country* or *The Age of Innocence*. The action of *The House of Mirth* occurs in the first years of the twentieth century, several stages and a few decades beyond the dispossession of old New York. We barely see any representatives of the faded aristocracy; what we do see in the first half of the book are several of its distant offshoots and descendants, most of them already tainted by the vulgarity of the new bourgeoisie yet, for no very good reasons, still contemptuous of it. The standards of those characters who have any claim to the old aristocracy are not so much guides to their own conduct as strategies for the exclusion of outsiders. Like Gus Trenor, they have kept some pretense to social superiority but very little right to it, and even an exceptional figure like Lawrence Selden, who does try to live by cultivated standards, has been forced into a genteel bohemianism and an acceptance of his failure to act with manly decisiveness.

In no way is the old aristocracy, or even the *idea* of the old aristocracy, held up as a significant model for behavior. Indeed, in *The House of Mirth* the moral positives seem almost disembodied, hovering like ghosts over the figures of Lily Bart and Lawrence Selden. When the new rich make their assault upon the world of the established rich, there occurs a brief contest between an aspiring and an entrenched snobbism, and soon enough, as one might expect, a truce is struck. The victim of that truce is Lily Bart.

Each step in Lily's decline allows Mrs. Wharton to examine the moral ugliness of still another segment of the wealthy classes. In the novel Lily begins with

The Trenors, who maintain a pretense of loyalty to traditional styles and values, even while frequently violating them. That they feel obliged to keep up this pretense does, however, have a restraining influence upon their conduct. Gus Trenor may harass Lily, but she can still appeal successfully to his sense of being a gentleman ("old habits . . . the hand of inherited order . . ."). Once dropped by the Trenors—a major sign she is slipping—Lily finds a place with

The Dorsets, who are at least as rich and socially powerful as the Trenors but in Mrs. Wharton's hierarchy occupy a lower rung. They no longer pretend to care about traditional styles and values. Bertha Dorset is a ferocious bitch, her husband a limp dyspeptic. They ruthlessly abandon Lily and she, no longer able to stay afloat in her familiar element, must now turn to the new rich. She does this with the help of

Carrie Fisher, a brilliantly portrayed figure who acts as guide for those *arrivistes* willing to pay for their social acceptance. Frankly materialistic, yet likable for her candor, Mrs. Fisher is troubled neither by Lily's scruples nor her delusions, and for a time she arranges that Lily find refuge with

The Brys, very rich and feverishly on the make. Gus Trenor may sneer when the Brys give their expensive "crush," but he goes and thereby helps to seal the fusion between his set and all that the Brys represent. Unable or unwilling to remain with the Brys, Lily finds a haven of sorts with

The Gormers, who also have large amounts of money but care less for status than pleasure. Once, however, Mrs. Gormer is tempted socially by the poisonous Bertha Dorset, Lily finds herself displaced again and must take refuge with

Norma Hatch, the wealthy divorcee who lives in a chaos of indolence, forever a prey to sharpers and schemers. Lily finds this atmosphere intolerable, and nothing remains for her but the last fall into the abyss of poverty.

As Lily goes down step by step, two figures stand on the sidelines observing her and occasionally troubling to intervene, but never decisively, never with full heart or unqualified generosity. Selden feels an acute sympathy for her, but a sympathy marred by fastidiousness; he loves her, but except for the last moment, not with a love prepared to accept the full measure of its risks. Rosedale sees her as a possible asset for his social climb and later finds himself vaguely moved by her troubles, but at the end he turns away, convinced she has lost her market value. Selden's ethical perceptions are as superior to Lily's as Rosedale's are inferior, but Mrs. Wharton, with her corrosive and thrusting irony, places the two men in a relationship of symmetrical exposure. In Mrs. Wharton's world men are often weak, either too refined for action or too coarse for understanding: they fail one, they do not come through . . . Lily ends her days alone.

III

The social setting of *The House of Mirth* is elaborated with complete assurance: one is always persuaded of the tangibility of Mrs. Wharton's milieu, the precision with which she observes nuances of status and place. But what finally draws and involves us is the personal drama enacted within this setting. Lily Bart is a victim of taste, both good and bad: she has a natural taste for moral and esthetic refinements which causes her to be repelled by the world of the rich, and she has an acquired taste for luxury that can be satisfied only in that world. She is too fine in her perceptions to act ruthlessly enough to achieve her worldly aims, and too much the captive of those aims to be able to live by her perceptions. She has enough moral awareness to respect civilized structures of behavior, but not enough moral courage to abandon the environment in which they are violated. She is trapped in a heart struggle between the pleasures of this world, that is, to lure the dismal millionaire Gryce into marriage, and the refinements of personal relations, which means to drop Gryce for the privilege of walking with Lawrence Selden on a Sunday afternoon. She pays, in the words of Percy Lubbock, "for her fastidiousness by finding herself abandoned by the vivid crowd: and she pays for her courtship of the crowd, so carefully taught her by all the conditions of life, by discovering that her independence is only strong enough to destroy and not to re-make her life."

Simply as an example of imaginative portraiture, Lily Bart is one of the triumphs of American writing. Mrs. Wharton has succeeded in that supremely difficult task of the novelist: to show a figure in plasticity and vibration while preserving the firm outlines of her conception. We soon grasp the nature of Lily's character, yet are repeatedly surprised and moved by its local shadings. Mrs. Wharton does not for a moment soften the judgments that Lily invites, nor does she hesitate to expose all of Lily's weakness and self-indulgence. Lily "was fond of pictures and flowers, and of sentimental fiction, and she could not help thinking that the possession of such tastes ennobled her desire for worldly advantage." And a still more biting sentence: "Selden's reputed civilization was generally regarded as a slight obstacle to easy intercourse, but Lily, who prided herself on her broad-minded recognition of literature, and always carried an Omar Khayyam in her traveling-bag, was attracted by this attribute, which she felt would have had its distinction in an older society." Through a steady accumulation of incidents Mrs. Wharton makes it clear that Lily is pitifully lacking in any core of personal being. At home neither in the Trenor mansion nor Selden's book-lined rooms nor the shabby apartment of her cousin Gerty Farish, Lily is at the mercy of her restlessness, a strangely disabling kind of restlessness which marks an unfinished self. Yet all of these judgments are stated or implied by Mrs. Wharton with a profound compassion, a sense of the sadness that comes to one in observing a lovely human being dash herself against the rocks of her own bewilderment. If Lily cannot maintain those flashes of self-awareness that come to her in moments of failure, she is still a generous and warm-hearted woman, open, in Mrs. Wharton's magnificent phrase, to "one of those sudden shocks of pity that sometimes decentralize a life."

Lily's fall is treated partly as a naturalistic drama in which a victim of circumstance is slowly crushed. She admires Selden because

> he had preserved . . . a happy air of viewing the show objectively, of having points of contact outside the great gilt cage . . . How alluring the world outside the cage appeared to Lily, as she heard its door clang on her! In reality, as she knew, the door never clanged: it stood always open; but most of the captives were like flies in a bottle, and having once flown in, could never regain their freedom.

This sense of fatality in *The House of Mirth* is reinforced, step by step, as Lily confronts the social demarcations of her world. Mrs. Wharton in her autobiography would later provide a first-rate description of this aspect of the book. In what ways, she asks herself, "could a society of irresponsible pleasure-seekers be said to have, on the 'old woes of the world,' any deeper bearing than the people composing such a society could guess?" And she answers: "A frivolous society can acquire dramatic significance only through what its frivolity destroys. Its tragic implication lies in its power of debasing people and ideas." Thus regarded, the ordeal of Lily Bart continues to be a significant one, even if its terms and setting have come to seem historically dated. In one way or another, the problem of mediating between the expectations of a commercial society and the ideals of humane civilization is not exactly unknown to us; only on the surface is our society so very different from that of Lily Bart.

This view of the novel is not accepted, however, by certain critics who question whether Lily's fate is very important or deeply affecting, and who see in her story little more than the malaise of an idle woman unable to dispense with privileges. In a phrase of dismissal Henry Seidel Canby has written of *The House of Mirth* that "it reveals nothing in the history of Lily Bart which wealth would not cure." He is wrong; exactly the opposite is true. Mrs. Wharton goes to some pains to stress that wealth lies within Lily's grasp if only she will do what she cannot bring herself to do: make sacrifices of taste, forgo assumptions of honor, accept conditions of tedium. That Lily yearns for wealth is obvious; that anyone could suppose it to be a "cure" for her is astonishing. But apart from his inaccuracy, Mr. Canby's statement displays a somewhat comic complacence: he writes as if the pressures of financial need had nothing to do with human suffering in our time, as if true tragedy were something apart from the hustle of daily life, and as if literary critics never worked themselves into a moral corner through a conflict between desires and standards. Lily Bart, to be sure, is not a heroine in the grand style: she is a weak and lovely woman. Her life, torn apart by what Mrs. Wharton calls "the eternal struggle between man's contending impulses," may not satisfy the Aristotelian concept of tragedy. But to say this is perhaps nothing more than to suggest how limited a value there is in applying such concepts to modern literature.

In any case, our response to Lily can hardly be exhausted by the sum of moral judgments we make about her. Once all statements of discount have been entered against Lily, we remain concerned and stirred by her effort—who has not known or experienced similar ones?—to bring together irreconcilable ways of life. Before the pathos of her failure, judgment fades into love.

IV

The House of Mirth is not written in the kind of prose, favored in many twentieth-century novels, that aims to resemble a transparent glass, a clear window upon the action. Mrs. Wharton's prose solicits attention in its own right. It asks us constantly to be aware of an authorial voice speaking with a full readiness to provide comment and generalization. At various points in the novel we are allowed some entrance into Lily Bart's mind, but never to the point of forgetting that it is Mrs. Wharton who guides us there and will soon be guiding us away. We are always conscious that the narrative comes to us through a style of high polish, austere irony, epigrammatic conciseness. What Mrs. Wharton says in her own right is just as much a part of the texture of the novel as the action and the dialogue.

Her style impresses one by its capacity for severe qualifications. Here is Mrs. Wharton on Bertha Dorset:

> She was smaller and thinner than Lily Bart, with a restless pliability of pose, as if she could have been crumpled up and run through a ring, like the sinuous draperies she affected. Her small pale face seemed the mere setting of a pair of dark exaggerated eyes, of which the visionary gaze contrasted curiously with her self-assertive tone and gestures; so that, as one of her friends observed, she was like a disembodied spirit who took up a great deal of room.

The writing here is extremely vivid, partly as a visual description of Bertha Dorset, but primarily as a generalized evocation of Mrs. Wharton's sense and judgment of her. There are numerous other examples that might be given for this power of concise and neat generalization. One remembers, as a comic instance, the sentence about Lily's dreary aunt: "Mrs. Peniston thought the country lonely and trees damp, and cherished a vague fear of meeting a bull." Or an instance of Mrs. Wharton's gift for dramatic summation: "It was success that dazzled [Lily]—she could distinguish facts plainly enough in the twilight of failure." Or Mrs. Wharton's capacity for a kind of statement that pertains both to the matter in hand and larger issues of human experience: Gerty Farish, pleased that Lily has contributed to a charity, "supposed her beautiful friend to be actuated by the same motive as herself—that sharpening of the moral vision which makes all human suffering so near and insistent that the other aspects of life fade into remoteness."

But even as one comes to savor the crispness of Mrs. Wharton's prose, there are passages in *The House of Mirth* that leave one uneasy. Usually these are passages in which she reveals the unfortunate tendency toward ladies'-magazine rhetoric that broke out in her later years. And usually they are passages in which she must confront a theme—the satisfactions of romantic love—she finds either too embarrassing or too upsetting to handle with ease. Writing about an encounter between Selden and Lily, she composes a sentence that, at least in its second clause, seems decidedly forced: "it was one of those moments when neither seemed to speak deliberately, when an indwelling voice in each called to the other across unsounded depths of feeling." Here is Mrs. Wharton's description of the last talk between Selden and Lily, utterly right in its first sentence and a purple lapse in the second:

> Something in truth lay dead between them—the love she had killed in him and could no longer call to life. But something lived between them also, and leaped up in her like an imperishable flame: it was the love his love had kindled, the passion of her soul for his.

To notice this stylistic problem is to approach a central limitation of Mrs. Wharton's writing. She knew only too well how experience can grind men into hopelessness, how it can leave them persuaded that the need for choice contains in itself the seeds of tragedy and the impossibility of choice the sources of pain. Everything that denies human desires, everything that reveals the power of the conditioned, everything that shreds and mocks our aspirations, she brought to full novelistic life. Where she failed was in giving imaginative embodiment to the human will to resist defeat or move beyond it. She lacked the unshakable serenity, the glow of transcendence, which illuminates even the most depressing of Henry James's novels. She lacked his ability to summon in commanding images of conduct the purity of children and the selflessness of girls; she had, in short, no vocabulary for happiness. Her work overwhelms us with its harsh truths, but finally it seems incomplete and earth-bound. Mrs. Wharton believed firmly in the moral positives she had inherited, but she could seldom project them into her work; all too often they survive only in terms of their violation. Hence the grinding, unrelenting, impatient tone of her work as if she sensed some deficiency, perhaps in the very scheme of things or only in her own vision, and did not know how to fill the need. Mrs. Wharton was a thoroughly conservative writer but there are times one is inclined to say, a bit paradoxically, that she is too hard on the rich, too glacial in her contempt for their mediocrity, too willing to slash away at them because she does not know anyone else to turn toward or against.

Such difficulties occur to one mainly in retrospect. When one reads and submits to the urgencies of a novel like *The House of*

Mirth, the effect is that of being held in a steady, inexorable enclosure. Mrs. Wharton's sense of the inescapability of waste—the waste of spirit, the waste of energy, the waste of beauty—comes to seem a root condition of human life. In her autobiography she wrote, "life is the saddest thing there is, next to death," and the best of her novels force us to entertain the possibility she is right.

Babbitt
by Sinclair Lewis, 1922

The critical reception of Babbitt *in 1922 was almost universally enthusiastic, but according to biographer Mark Schorer the review that seemed to mean the most to Lewis was this one by British author and journalist Rebecca West as it appeared in* The New Statesman.

M*ain Street* was a good book. One was as glad that it attained the incredibly tremendous triumph of being an American best-seller as one might be when a thoroughly nice girl wins the Calcutta Sweepstake. But on reading *Main Street* one did not in the least feel as if one were dancing round a bonfire. Heat and light and exhilaration were foreign to the hour. It was a sincere, competent, informative, even occasionally passionate piece of writing, but it had not that something extra and above the logical treatment of its subject—that "peacock's feather in the cap," as Yeats has called it—which makes the work of art. Moreover, it had not much in it of its author's own quality, and that was felt as a serious deprivation by those who were acquainted with Mr. Lewis and his literary past, by those who knew, for example, of the entertaining investigation into spiritualism he conducted on behalf of one of the American magazines. (During the course of this, swathing with seriousness a remarkable personal appearance which bears a strong resemblance to that of Mr. George Grossmith, but made more glorious with red hair, he sat down beside many mediums and asked chokingly for a message from his "dear friend, Mr. H. G. Wells, the English novelist, who recently passed over"; and usually got one.) But these deficiencies are rectified in *Babbitt*. It has that something extra, over and above, which makes the work of art, and it is signed in every line with the unique personality of the writer. It is saturated with America's vitality which makes one obey the rhythms of its dance music, which gives unlimited power over audiences to their actresses whether they be artistically dog-lazy like Ethel Levey, or negligible like Peggy O'Neill. And combined with this, Mr. Lewis has an individual gift of humour, a curiously sage devotion to craftsmanship, and a poetic passion for his own, new country.

To write satire is to perform a miracle. One must hate the world so much that one's hatred strikes sparks, but one must hate it only because it disappoints one's invincible love of it; one must write in denunciation of ugliness and put the thing down in unmistakable black and white, yet keep this, as all written things, within the sphere of beauty. But Mr. Lewis has been equal to these things. He writes of vulgar Zenith City and its vulgar children, yet never writes a vulgar line. He is merciless to George F. Babbitt, that standardised child of that standardised city, with his pad-cheeks and his puffy hands, his hypocrisy and his ignorance, his dishonesty and his timid sensualities; and he reveals him lovable and pitiable, a strayed soul disconsolate through frustrated desires for honour and beauty. He can flame into transports of exasperation with the religion of business and its paunchy priesthood—marvellous transports these are, for what we have here is the Celt getting angry with the Englishman. For Zenith City and Babbitt are amazingly English. They represent that section of America which seems the least affected by the Latin and Jewish and Celtic leavens; the resemblance of kinship is patent, even blatant. Oh, never star was lost here but it rose afar! Look West where whole new thousands are! In Zenith City what Leverhulme! And the Celt in the person of Mr. Lewis cannot bear it. Vindictively he reports their flat, endlessly repetitive, excessively and simultaneously ignorant and sophisticated conversation at dinner parties and in smoking-cars. He snatches out of the paper enraged parodies of the *Poemulations* they read instead of poetry—by T. Cholmondeley Frink, who was not only the author of *Poemulations,* which, syndicated daily in sixty-

seven leading newspapers, gave him one of the largest audiences of
any poet in the world, but also an optimistic lecturer and the creator
of "Ads. that Add."

> I sat alone and groused and thunk, and scratched my head and sighed
> and wunk and groaned. There still are boobs, alack, who'd like the old
> time gin-mill back; that den, that makes a sage a loon, the vile and smelly
> old saloon! I'll never miss their poison booze, whilst I the bubbling spring
> can use, that leaves my head at merry morn as clear as any babe new-
> born!

He describes with deadly malice the proceedings at the lunch of
the Zenith Boosters' Club. "The International Organisation of
Boosters' Clubs has become a world-force for optimism, manly pleas-
antry, and good business." Its members all wore a button marked
"Boosters—Pep!" At each place at the lunch-table, on the famous
day when George F. Babbitt was elected Vice-President, was laid
a present, a card printed in artistic red and black:

> SERVICE AND BOOSTERISM.
> Service finds its finest opportunity and development only in its broad-
> est and deepest application and the consideration of its perpetual action
> upon reaction. I believe the highest type of Service, like the most
> progressive tenets of ethics, senses unceasingly and is motived by ac-
> tive adherence and loyalty to that which is the essential principle of
> Boosterism—Good Citizenship in all its factors and aspects.
> DAD PETERSEN.
> Compliments of Dadbury Petersen Advertising Corp.
> "Ads not Fads at Dads."

"The Boosters all read Mr. Petersen's aphorism and said they understood it perfectly."

Yet behind all this is a truth. There is something happening in
among these hustling congregations of fat and absurd men. The
present condition of George F. Babbitt may be discomfortable.
Loathing at the smooth surface of his standardised life, destitute
of interstices that might admit romance, may move him to vain
and painful flights towards the promise of light; to his comical
attempts to find spiritual comfort in the Chatham Street Presby-
terian Church; to his efforts to make a synthetic substitute for love

out of the kittenish contacts of Mrs. Tanis Judique. ("And shall I call you George? Don't you think it's awfully nice when two people have so much—what shall I say?—analysis that they can discard all these conventions and understand each other and become acquainted right away, like ships that pass in the night?") Little as he has, he yet possesses a promise. The value of that possession can be estimated by comparing Babbitt with his English analogue, Sir Gerald Doak, whom Mr. Lewis shows, touring the States in a state of panic because a title bought by the accumulations of industry in Nottingham brings on him the attentions of earnest hostesses who (misled by their conception of the British aristocracy) talk to him about polo and the galleries of Florence. Paunch for paunch these two sound business men seem much the same. But there is for Babbitt a certain advantage; or perhaps, in the transitional and blundering state of affairs revealed in this book, it should be called a certain opportunity. He moves in a setting so vast and so magnificent that surely it must ultimately dictate vastness and magnificence to the action it contains. There are in this volume a few pages, which must be counted among the masterpieces of satire; they profess to give a verbatim report of the speech delivered by Mr. George F. Babbitt at the Annual Dinner of The Zenith Real Estate Board. In it Mr. Lewis's exasperation rises to the pitch of genius. It dances on the chest of Babbitt's silly standardised self and his silly standardised world. There is one absurd passage, when Babbitt cries:

"With all modesty, I want to stand up here as a representative businessman and gently whisper, 'Here's our kind of folks! Here's the specifications of the standardised American Citizen! Here's the new generation of Americans: fellows with hair on their chests and smiles in their eyes and adding machines in their offices. . . . So! In my clumsy way I have tried to sketch the Real He-man, the fellow with Zep and Bang! And it's because Zenith has so large a proportion of such men, that it's the most stable, the greatest of our cities. New York also has its thousands of Real Folks, but New York is cursed with unnumbered foreigners. So are Chicago and San Francisco. Oh, we have a golden roster of cities—Detroit and Cleveland with their renowned factories. Cincinnati with its great machine-tool and soap products, Pittsburgh and

Birmingham with their steel, Kansas City and Minneapolis and Omaha that open their bountiful gates on the bosom of the ocean-like wheatlands, and countless other magnificent sister-cities, for by the last census, there were no less than sixty-eight glorious American burgs with a population of over one hundred thousand! And all these cities stand together for power and purity, and against foreign ideas and communism. Atlanta with Hartford, Rochester with Denver, Milwaukee with Indianapolis, Los Angeles with Scranton, Portland, Maine, with Portland, Oregon. A good live-wire from Baltimore, or Seattle or Duluth is the twin brother of every like fellow booster from Buffalo or Akron, Fort Worth or Oskaloosa!"

It is a bonehead Walt Whitman speaking. Stuffed like a Christmas goose as Babbitt is, with silly films, silly newspapers, silly talk, silly oratory, there has yet struck him the majestic creativeness of his own country, its miraculous power to bear and nourish without end countless multitudes of men and women. He is so silly, so ill-educated (though as he says, "the State University is my own Alma Mater, and I am proud to be known as an alumni") that he prefers to think of it bearing and nourishing countless multitudes of featureless standardised Regular Guys. But there is in these people a vitality so intense that it must eventually bolt with them and land them willy-nilly into the sphere of intelligence; and this immense commercial machine will become the instrument of their aspiration.

Before he followed his wife, Babbitt stood at the westernmost window of their room. This residential settlement, Floral Heights, was on a rise; and though the centre of the city was three miles away—Zenith had between three and four hundred thousand inhabitants now—he could see the top of the Second National Tower, an Indiana limestone building of thirty-five storeys.

Its shining wall rose against April sky to a simple cornice like a streak of white fire. Integrity was in the tower, and decision. It bore its strength lightly as a tall soldier. As Babbitt stared, the nervousness was soothed from his face, his slack chin lifted in reverence. All he articulated was, "That's one lovely sight!" but he was inspired by the rhythm of the city; his love of it renewed. He beheld the tower as a temple-spire of the religion of business, a faith passionate, exalted, surpassing common men; and as he clumped down to breakfast he whistled the ballad, "Oh, by gee, by gosh, by jingo," as though it were a hymn melancholy and noble.

H. L. MENCKEN ON

An American Tragedy
by Theodore Dreiser, 1925

Newspaper editor and social commentator H. L. Mencken was a friend of Dreiser's for almost forty years. This introduction was written for the Memorial edition of An American Tragedy, *which was published in 1946, a year after Dreiser's death.*

The prototype of Clyde Griffiths was a young man named Chester E. Gillette who drowned a girl named Grace Brown in a lake in Herkimer county on July 11, 1906, and was electrocuted for it on March 20, 1908. This may seem a strange way to introduce a work presumably of the imagination, but I suspect that the nascent Ph.D.'s who labor Dreiser and his novels hereafter will have to resort to it pretty often, for all of those novels are based upon things actually seen, heard or heard of, and not a few of them come close to the literal reporting of the last chapters of *An American Tragedy*. Dreiser, indeed, was probably the most matter-of-fact novelist ever known on earth. It was seldom that he departed from what he understood to be the record, and he never did so willingly. I recall a curious example in the days when *The "Genius"* was under fire by the Comstocks, and all the friends of its author were cooperating in efforts to deliver him from their clutches. I was told off, at one stage, to enter upon negotiations with old Anthony's successor, a lawyer by the name of Sumner, in the hope of inducing him to let up on the book at the cost of a few minor changes. I found this Sumner an amiable fellow, and we quickly drew up a sort of protocol by which he waived most of his objections, but insisted that a word here or there should be expunged or a situation toned down a bit. One of these situations, as I recall it, depicted Eugene Witla, the hero, as thrusting an inquisitive hand up a girl's skirt. This was in 1922 and the case against *The "Genius"* had been going on for six long years, so I was glad enough to agree to stop the explorer at the patella in order to get the book released, and Dreiser restored to royalties and peace of mind. But I was reckoning without the conscience of a really implacable respecter of facts. He agreed under pressure to other changes that seemed to me to be quite as important to the flow of the narrative, but when it came to this one he was a stone wall. I could see no logic in his objection, which quickly became violent, and said so. "But that," he declared finally and immovably, "is something I simply can't consent to. It *really happened.*" So the episode remained in the book, and presently, when the Comstocks subsided, the presses began to roll again, and if the plates haven't worn out Eugene is still groping—an operation considered scandalous in 1922, but now somewhat shorn of its old horrors.

Here, as in many another place, Dreiser himself was his own hero. He had a mind closely packed with trivia that were not trivial at all, and he poured them into all his books. When he described a street in Chicago and New York it was always a street that he knew as intimately as the policeman on the beat, and he never omitted any detail that had stuck in his mind—a queer sign, a shopkeeper standing in his doorway, a leaky fireplug, an ashcan, a stray dog. When he sent some character into an eating-house for a meal it was always some eating-house that he had been to himself, and the meal he described in such relentless detail was one he had eaten, digested and remembered. Coming to the departure or arrival of a train, he commonly gave the precise time, and it could be verified by the railroad schedule. Nearly all the people of his novels were people he had known, man and woman alike. Clyde Griffiths in *An American Tragedy* is not only Chester E. Gillette; he is also a bell-boy encountered in Chicago, and diligently pumped of his so-called ideas. The father of this poor fish, the street preacher, is not first seen in Kansas City by chance: he is placed there because that is where Dreiser found him, far back in 1891 or 1892. I first

heard of him in 1910 or thereabout, at which time he figured in a
first sketch of the book that was to appear finally, more than thirty-
five years later, as *The Bulwark*. Why he was transferred to *An
American Tragedy* I do not know, for in the days when it was under
way I was seeing very little of his historian, but I recall him clearly
over all these years, for it was a peculiarity of Dreiser that his
characters always lingered in memory, even when his stories faded.

I spent the better part of forty years trying to induce him to
reform and electrify his manner of writing, but so far as I am aware
with no more effect than if I had sought to persuade him to take
up golf or abandon his belief in non-Euclidian arcana. The defects
of his style, of course, have been somewhat exaggerated by a long
line of literary popinjays, including myself; he was quite capable,
on occasion, of writing simply and even gracefully, as you will
discover if you turn to Chapter XIII of Book III of the present tale.
Nevertheless, his was predominantly viscous writing, and not in-
frequently its viscosity was increased by clichés and counter-words
that pulled up the reader in an extremely painful manner. In *The
"Genius"* he performed inhuman barbarities upon the dubious word
trig, and in *An American Tragedy* he does the same with *chic*. His
method of work was not unlike that of a man in a dream—even
something like that of a spiritualist calling off the messages of Wah-
wah, the Indian chief. He would sit down to his desk, in the days
when I saw him oftenest, and bang away with pen and ink for four
or five hours. The stuff poured out of him almost automatically: it
was, as I have said, mainly reminiscence. If he stopped at all, it
was to go to the library to verify a street-name, or to find out when
the Pennsylvania Railroad first reached McKeesport, or to establish
the precise date of the *General Slocum* disaster. So slaving away,
he would produce 3,000 words by mid-afternoon, and then he would
go for a walk, usually alone. His evenings were given over to what
he regarded as social relaxation. That is to say, he would sit almost
in silence, gloomily folding and refolding his handkerchief while
some propagandist for a new and bizarre cult tried to recruit him,
or a woman visitor entertained him with tales of the scoundrelism
of her husband, or a young author read bad poetry to him. He was

very kind to this last class, and tackled publishers and editors in behalf of many—a few of them good ones, but the rest only Greenwich Village mountebanks. He had very little critical sense, either for his own work or for that of others, and some of the aspirants who got his help deserved the gallows instead.

His mind, as I have said, was packed to suffocation with facts directly observed, but he got, I think, relatively little out of books, for he was not a heavy reader in those days, and what he read was not always of authority. The massive effect that Huxley and Spencer had had upon him in early life sufficed to keep him hostile to the Catholic piety of his father to his dying day, but he remained of a generally believing cast of mind, and was easily fetched by secular theologies. When the Freudian revelation dawned upon the Republic he resisted it only faintly, and was presently suffering from what he himself once described in my presence as a complex complex. There are traces of it in *An American Tragedy*: he even tries to account for the imbecility of judges and district attorneys in terms of infantile suppressions. But the book is much more heavily marked by the "chemic" theory of human behavior that entertained him during the twenties. Where he picked it up I do not know: perhaps he invented it himself. Whatever its source, it made him, for a time, a complete fatalist, even a sort of Calvinist, and hence a nihilist in the domain of morals. It was this nihilism, I believe, that brought down the Comstocks upon *The "Genius"* rather than any dirtiness in the text. That text, in truth, was extraordinarily free from indecent words and naughty innuendoes, as I discovered when I went through it word for word, seeking to get the Comstocks off his back. His heirs and assigns among American novelists have gone very much further, and yet escaped the challenging whistles of Christian watchmen. It will probably astound posterity to hear that even *An American Tragedy* was forbidden as obscene in Boston. It is, in fact, no more obscene than a table of stock prices. But it is undoubtedly profoundly immoral, for if it teaches anything at all it is that committing a murder is a sort of biological accident, like breaking a leg or becoming a father.

This book was Dreiser's greatest success, and for a brief space it made him rich, as he himself understood riches. He moved out of the slum where he had lived for many years, acquired a somewhat pretentious apartment, and later added a house in a more or less swanky suburb. But I doubt that this exalted scale of living was ever really comfortable to him, and I suspect that he was rather glad of it when the money began to run low and he returned to simpler ways. He was the sort of man who had few wants and none of them luxurious. In the days when *The Financier, The Titan* and *The "Genius"* were under way he lived in dingy quarters in Tenth Street, and took his meals in the modest establishments of the vicinity. Many's the time I saw him glow with delight over a *rôtisserie* fowl, presumably a chicken, and a bottle of red wine from Hoboken, N. J. He had a great many friends, and was respected in his own craft for his adamantine integrity: few other novelists in history have endured so much for the sake of personal principle and artistic conscience. As I have noted, he was very kind to young authors, and went to great pains to help them. In my days as a magazine editor he sent dozens of them to me, and it always gave him pain when I had to report that this or that one was a jackass. Once I was sitting in his house, along with four or five well-known writers of the day, when there was a loud knocking at the door, which opened directly upon the front steps, for the apartment was on the ground floor. When Dreiser went to the door a somewhat intoxicated young man thrust a bottle of champagne at him, and brushed his way in. Dreiser had never seen this young man before, but received him politely and inquired his business. The visitor then introduced himself, and said that the bottle of champagne was his pious offering to an elder he admired. He was a newcomer who had written a book of great promise and was destined to go far before an early death cut him short. Dreiser let him monopolize the conversation, and treated him with the greatest deference. Years later one of the other men present was translated to Heaven, and his friends printed what purported to be an autobiography of him. In it the statement appeared that Dreiser had turned the intruding young man out of the house. It would be hard to imagine a less probable story. Indeed, it is impossible to think of Dreiser kicking *any* one out of his house, save maybe some wandering archbishop. I have even seen him offer his hospitality to publishers, a class of men he grouped with kidnapers, dope-fiends and pirates on the high seas.

Whether or not *An American Tragedy* will survive in the Dreiser canon is a question that can be answered only by time. It was, as I have said, his greatest success while he lived, but at least a part of that success, I suspect, was due to its sheer bulk. The reading public always embraces long and thick novels, for its members, on the lower and more numerous levels, read only one or two books a year, and they like something that will last them all Winter. If any reader of the present volume is pressed for time, I advise him to begin his reading with the second book. The first is a menagerie of all Dreiser's worst deficiencies, but in the second he becomes again the adept and persuasive reporter. The last scenes have in them all the plausibility that made *Sister Carrie* a memorable event in American letters. To be sure, they stick close to the record— but surely not over-close. It is Dreiser who is telling the story, not some commonplace reporter. It offers a picture of profound tragedy seen through a suitably melancholy temperament. The author's brooding, noted by so many critics incapable of inventing a better word, is all over it. It is not only a minutely detailed picture of one unhappy young man's life; it is a commentary upon human life in general. Dreiser, in the days when the story was written, saw that life as predominantly hopeless and meaningless. This was the note of all his earlier novels. In his old age, with his faculties dimming, he revolted against his own philosophy, and embraced the glittering promises of the Marxian gospel. But in *An American Tragedy* he was still content to think of the agonies of mankind as essentially irremediable, and to lay them, not to the sins of economic royalists, but to the blind blundering of the God responsible for complexes, suppressions, hormones and vain dreams.

MALCOLM COWLEY ON

The Great Gatsby
by F. Scott Fitzgerald, 1925

The literary situation in the twenties interested editor and literary historian Malcolm Cowley throughout his writing career, qualifying him in a special way to introduce the novelist and the book most identified with that decade to a new generation of readers. His introduction to The Great Gatsby, *entitled "The Romance of Money," appeared in the Scribner's edition of 1953.*

Although Fitzgerald regarded himself, and was regarded by others, as a representative figure of the age, there was one respect in which he did not represent most of its serious writers. In that respect he was much closer to the men of his college year who were trying to get ahead in the business world; like them he was fascinated by the process of earning and spending money. The young businessmen of his time were bitterly determined to be successful and, much more than their successors of a later generation, they had been taught to measure success, failure, and even virtue in monetary terms. They had learned in school and Sunday school that virtue was rewarded with money and that viciousness was punished by the loss of money; apparently their only problem was to earn lots of it fast. Yet money was merely a convenient and inadequate symbol for what they dreamed of earning. The best of them were like Jay Gatsby in having "some heightened sensitivity to the promise of life"; or they were like another Fitzgerald hero, Dexter Green—of "Winter Dreams"— who "wanted not association with glittering things and glittering people—he wanted the glittering things themselves." Their real dream was that of achieving a new status and a new essence, of rising to a loftier place in the mysterious hierarchy of human worth.

The serious writers also dreamed of rising to a loftier status, but—except for Fitzgerald—they felt that money-making was the wrong way to rise. They liked money if it reached them in the form of gifts or legacies or publishers' advances, but they were afraid of high earned incomes because of what the incomes stood for: obligations, respectability, time lost from their own work, expensive habits that would drive them to earn still higher incomes; in short, a series of involvements in the commercial culture that was hostile to art. "If you want to ruin a writer," I used to hear them saying, "just give him a big magazine contract or a job at ten thousand a year." Many of them tried to preserve their independence by earning only enough to keep them alive while writing; a few liked to regard themselves as heroes of poverty and failure.

Their attitude toward money went into the texture of their work, which was noncommercial in the sense of being written in various new styles that the public was slow to accept. The 1920s were the great age of literary experiment, when the new writers were moving in all directions simultaneously. Some of them tried to capture in words the effects of modern painting (like E. E. Cummings); some used the older literary language with Shakespearean orotundity (like Thomas Wolfe); some worked at developing a new language based on Midwestern speech (like Hemingway). Some tried to omit all but the simplest adjectives (again like Hemingway); some used five or six long adjectives in a row (like Faulkner); some ran adjectives and adverbs together in a hurryconfusing fashion (like Dos Passos). Some approached their characters only from the outside, some gave only their inmost thoughts, their streams of subconsciousness, some broke a story into fragments, some told it backwards, some tried to dispense with stories. They were all showing the same spirit of adventure and exploration in fiction that their contemporaries were showing in the business world. That spirit made them part of the age, but at the same time they were trying to criticize and escape from it, and many of them looked back longingly to other ages when, so they liked to think, artists had wealthy patrons and hence were able to live outside the economic system.

Fitzgerald, on the other hand, immersed himself in the age and always remained close to the business world which the others were trying to evade. That world was the background of his stories and they performed a business function in themselves, by supplying the narration that readers followed like a thread through the labyrinth of advertising in the slick-paper magazines. He did not divorce himself from readers by writing experimental prose or by inventing new methods of telling or refusing to tell a story. His very real originality was a matter of mood and subject rather than form and it was more evident in his novels than in his stories, good as the stories often were. Although he despised the trade of writing for magazines—or despised it with part of his mind—he worked at it honestly. It yielded him a large income that he couldn't have earned in any other fashion and the income was necessary to his self-respect.

Fitzgerald kept an accurate record of his earnings—in the big ledger where he also recorded his deeds and misdeeds, as if to strike a book-keeper's balance between them—but he was always vague about his expenditures and was usually vague about his possessions, including his balance in the bank. Once he asked the cashier, "How much money have I got?" The cashier looked in a big book and answered without even scowling, "None." Fitzgerald resolved to be more thrifty, knowing that he would break the resolution. He had little interest in money for itself and less in the physical objects it would buy. On the other hand, he had a great interest in earning money, lots of it fast, because that was a sort of gold medal awarded with the blue ribbon for competitive achievement. Once the money was earned he and Zelda liked to spend lots of it fast, usually for impermanent things: not for real estate, fine motorcars, or furniture, but for traveling expenses, the rent of furnished houses, the wages of nurses and servants; for entertainments, party dresses, and feather fans of five colors. Zelda was as proudly careless about money as an eighteenth-century nobleman's heir. Scott was more practical and had his penny-pinching moments, as if in memory of his childhood, but at other times he liked to spend without counting in order to enjoy a sense of careless potency.

In his attitude toward money he revealed the new spirit of

an age when conspicuous accumulation was giving way to conspicuous earning and spending. It was an age when gold was melted down and became fluid; when wealth was no longer measured in possessions—land, houses, livestock, machinery—but rather in dollars per year, as a stream is measured by its flow; when for the first time the expenses of government were being met by income taxes more than by property and excise taxes. There were still old solid fortunes at the hardly accessible peak of the social system, which young men dreamed of reaching but the romantic figures of the age were not capitalists properly speaking. They were hired executives, promoters, salesmen, stock gamblers, or racketeers, and they were millionaires in a new sense—not men each of whom owned a million dollars' worth of property, but men who lived in rented apartments and had nothing but stock certificates and life-insurance policies (or nothing but credit and the proper connections), while spending more than the income of the old millionaires.

All these changes and survivals, as refracted through different personalities, are mirrored in Fitzgerald's work. In dealing with the romance of money, he chose the central theme of his American age. "Americans," he liked to say, "should be born with fins, and perhaps they were—perhaps money was a form of fin."

II

One of his remarks about his work has always puzzled his critics. "D. H. Lawrence's great attempt to synthesize animal and emotional—things he left out," Fitzgerald wrote in his notebook, then added the comment, "Essential pre-Marxian. Just as I am essentially Marxian." He was never Marxian in any sense of the word that Marxians of whatever school would be willing to accept. It is true that he finally read *Das Kapital* and was impressed by "the terrible chapter," as he called it, "on 'The Working Day' "; but it left in him not so much as a trace of Marx's belief in the mission of the proletariat.

His picture of proletarian life was of something alien to his background, mysterious and even criminal. It seems to have been symbolized in some of his stories by the riverfront strip in St. Paul that languished in the shadow of the big houses on the bluff; he described the strip as a gridiron of mean streets where consumptive or pugilistic youths lounged in front of poolrooms, their skins turned livid by the neon lights. In *The Great Gatsby* he must have been thinking about the lower levels of American society when he described the valley of ashes between West Egg and New York—"A fantastic farm," he called it, "where ashes grow like wheat into ridges and hills and grotesque gardens; where ashes take the forms of houses and chimneys and rising smoke and, finally, with a transcendent effort, of men who move dimly and always crumbling through the powdery air." One of his early titles for the novel was "Among Ash Heaps and Millionaires"—as if he were setting the two against each other while suggesting a vague affinity between them. Tom Buchanan, the brutalized millionaire, found a mistress in the valley of ashes.

In Fitzgerald's stories there could be no real struggle between this dimly pictured ash-gray proletariat and the bourgeoisie. On the other hand, there could be a different struggle that the author must have regarded, for a time, as essentially Marxian. It was the struggle that I have already suggested, between wealth as fluid income and wealth as a solid possession—or rather, since Fitzgerald is not an essayist but a story-teller, it is between a man and a woman as representatives of the new and the old moneyed classes.

We are not allowed to forget that they are representatives. The man comes from a family with little or no money, but he manages to attend an Eastern university—often Harvard or Yale, to set a distance between the hero and the Princeton author. He then sets out to earn a fortune equal to those of his wealthy classmates. Usually what he earns is not a fortune but an impressively large income, after he has become a success in his chosen profession—which may be engineering or architecture or advertising or the laundry business or bootlegging or real estate or even, in one story, frozen fish; the heroes are never writers like himself, although one of them is described as a popular dramatist. When the heroes are halfway to success, they fall in love.

The woman—or rather the girl—in a Fitzgerald story is younger

F. Scott Fitzgerald

and richer than the man and the author makes it even clearer that
she represents her social class. "She was a stalk of ripe corn," he
says of one heroine, "but bound not as cereals are but as a rare first
edition, with all the binder's art. She was lovely and expensive and
about nineteen." Of another heroine he says when she first appears
that "Her childish beauty was wistful and sad about being so rich
and sixteen." Later, when her father loses his money, the hero pays
her a visit in London. "All around her," Fitzgerald says, "he could
feel the vast Mortmain fortune melting down, seeping back into
the matrix whence it had come." The hero thinks that she might
marry him, now that she has fallen almost to his financial level;
but he finds that the Mortmain (or dead-hand) fortune, even though
lost, is still a barrier between them. Note that the man is not
attracted by the fortune in itself. He is not seeking money so much
as position at the peak of the social hierarchy and the girl becomes
the symbol of that position, the incarnation of its mysterious power.
That is Daisy Buchanan's charm for the great Gatsby, and it is the
reason why he directs his whole life toward winning back her love.

"She's got an indiscreet voice," Nick Carraway says of her. "It's
full of—" and he hesitates.

"Her voice is full of money," Gatsby says suddenly.

And Nick, the narrator, thinks to himself, "That was it. I'd
never understood before. It was full of money—that was the inexhaustible charm that rose and fell in it, the cymbals' song of it. . . .
High in a white palace the king's daughter, the golden girl."

In Fitzgerald's stories a love affair is like secret negotiations between the diplomats of two countries which are not at peace and not
quite at war. For a moment they forget their hostility, find it transformed into mutual curiosity, attraction, even passion (though the
passion is not physical); but the hostility will survive even in marriage,
if marriage is to be their future. I called the lovers diplomats,
ambassadors, and that is another way of saying that they are representatives. When they meet it is as if they were leaning toward each
other from separate high platforms—the man from a platform built
up of his former poverty, his ambition, his competitive triumphs, his
ability to earn and spend always more, more; the girl from another

platform covered with cloth of gold and feather fans of many colors, but beneath them a sturdy pile of stock certificates representing the ownership of mines, forests, factories, villages—all of Candy Town.

She is the embodied spirit of wealth, as can be clearly seen in one of the best of Fitzgerald's early stories, "Winter Dreams." A rising young man named Dexter Green takes home the daughter of a millionaire for whom he used to be a caddy. She is Judy Jones, "a slender enamelled doll in cloth of gold: gold in a band at her head, gold in two slipper points at her dress's hem." The rising young man stops his coupé, Fitzgerald says, "in front of the great white bulk of the Mortimer Jones house, somnolent, gorgeous, drenched with the splendor of the damp moonlight. Its solidity startled him. The strong walls, the steel of the girders, the breadth and beam and pomp of it were there only to bring out the contrast with the young beauty beside him. It was sturdy to accentuate her slightness—as if to show what a breeze could be generated by a butterfly's wing." Butterflies used to be taken as symbols of the soul. The inference is clear that, holding Judy in his arms, Dexter is embracing the spirit of a great fortune.

Nicole Warren, the heroine of *Tender Is the Night,* is the spirit of an even greater fortune. Fitzgerald says of her:

> Nicole was the product of much ingenuity and toil. For her sake trains began their run at Chicago and traversed the round belly of the continent to California; chicle factories fumed and link belts grew link by link in factories; men mixed toothpaste in vats and drew mouthwash out of copper hogsheads; girls canned tomatoes quickly in August or worked rudely at the five-and-tens on Christmas Eve; half-breed Indians toiled on Brazilian coffee plantations and dreamers were muscled out of patent rights in new tractors—these were some of the people who gave a tithe to Nicole, and as the whole system swayed and thundered onward it lent a feverish bloom to such processes of hers as wholesale buying [of luxuries], like the flush of a fireman's face holding his post before a spreading blaze.

Sometimes Fitzgerald's heroines are candid, even brutal, about class relationships. "Let's start right," the heroine of "Winter Dreams" says to Dexter Green on the first evening they spend alone together. "Who are you?"

"I'm nobody," Dexter tells her, without adding that he had been her father's caddy. "My career is largely a matter of futures."

"Are you poor?"

"No," he says frankly, "I'm probably making more money than any man my age in the Northwest. I know that's an obnoxious remark, but you advised me to start right."

"There was a pause," Fitzgerald adds. "Then she smiled and the corners of her mouth drooped and an almost imperceptible sway brought her closer to him, looking up into his eyes." Money brings them together, but later they are separated by something undefined—a mere whim of Judy's, it seems on one's first reading of the story, though one comes to feel that the whim was based on her feeling that she should marry a man of her own caste. Dexter, as he goes East to earn a still larger income, is filled with regret for "the country of illusions, of youth, of the richness of life, where his winter dreams had flourished." It seems likely that Judy Jones, like Josephine Perry in a series of later stories, was a character suggested by Fitzgerald's memories of a debutante with whom he was desperately in love during his first years at Princeton; afterward she made a more sensible marriage and Fitzgerald, too, regretted his winter dreams. As for the general attitude toward the rich that began to be expressed in the story, it is perhaps connected with his experiences in 1919, when Zelda broke off their engagement because they couldn't hope to live on his salary as a junior copywriter. Later he said of the time:

> During a long summer of despair I wrote a novel instead of letters, so it came out all right; but it came out all right for a different person. The man with the jingle of money in his pocket who married the girl a year later would always cherish an abiding distrust, an animosity, toward the leisure class—not the conviction of a revolutionist but the smoldering hatred of a peasant.

His mixture of feelings toward the very rich, which included curiosity and admiration as well as distrust, is revealed in his treatment of a basic situation that reappears in many of his stories. Of course he presented other situations that were not directly concerned with the relationship between social classes. He wrote about the problem of adjusting oneself to life, which he thought was especially difficult in the case of self-indulgent American women. He wrote about the manners of flappers and slickers. He wrote engagingly about his own boyhood. He wrote about the attempt to recapture youthful dreams, about the patching-up of broken marriages, about the contrast between Northern and Southern manners, about Americans going to pieces in Europe, about the self-tortures of gifted alcoholics, and in much of his later work—as notably in *The Last Tycoon*—he would be expressing his admiration for supremely great technicians, such as brain surgeons and movie directors. But a great number of his stories, especially the early ones, start with the basic situation I have mentioned: a rising young man of the middle class in love with the daughter of a very rich family. (Sometimes the family is Southern, in which case it needn't be so rich, since a high social status can exist in the South without great wealth.)

From that beginning the story may take any one of several turns. The hero may marry the girl, but only after she loses her fortune or (as in "Presumption" and " 'The Sensible Thing' ") he gains an income greater than hers. He may lose the girl (as in "Winter Dreams") and always remember that she represented his early aspirations. In "The Bridal Party" he resigns himself to the loss after being forced to recognize that the rich man she married is stronger and more capable than himself. In "More Than Just a House" he learns that the girl is empty and selfish and ends by marrying her good sister; in "The Rubber Check" he marries Ellen Mortmain's quiet cousin. There is, however, still another development out of the Fitzgerald situation that comes closer to revealing his ambiguous feelings toward the very rich. To state it simply—too simply—the rising young man wins the rich girl and then is destroyed by her wealth or her relatives.

The plot is like that of "Young Lochinvar," but with a tragic ending—as if fair Ellen's armed kinsmen had overtaken the pair, or as if they had slain the hero by treachery. Fitzgerald used it for the first time in a fantasy, "The Diamond as Big as the Ritz," which he wrote in St. Paul in the winter of 1921–1922. Like many other fantasies it reveals more of the author's mind than does his more realistic work. It deals with the adventures of a boy named John T. Unger (we might read "Hunger"), who was born in a town on the Mississippi called Hades, though it might also be called St. Paul. He is sent away to St. Midas', which is "the most expensive and most exclusive boys' preparatory school in the world," and there he meets a classmate named Percy Washington, who invites him to spend the summer at his home in the West. On the train Percy confides to him that his father is the richest man alive and owns a diamond bigger than the Ritz-Carlton Hotel (solid as opposed to fluid wealth).

The description of the Washington mansion, in its hidden valley that wasn't even shown on the maps of the U.S. Geodetic Survey, is fantasy mingled with burlesque; but then the familiar Fitzgerald note appears. John falls in love with Percy's younger sister, Kismine. After an idyllic summer Kismine tells him accidentally—she had meant to keep the secret—that he will very soon be murdered, like all the former guests of the Washingtons. "It was done very nicely," Kismine explains to him. "They were drugged while they were asleep—and their families were always told that they died of scarlet fever in Butte. . . . I shall probably have visitors too—I'll harden up to it. We can't let such an inevitable thing as death stand in the way of enjoying life while we have it. Think how lonesome it'd be out here if we never had *anyone*. Why, father and mother have sacrificed some of their best friends just as we have."

Tom and Daisy Buchanan also sacrificed some of their best friends. "They were careless people, Tom and Daisy—they smashed up things and creatures and then retreated back into their money or their vast carelessness, or whatever it was that kept them together, and let other people clean up the mess they had made." "The Diamond as Big as the Ritz" can have a happy ending for the two lovers because it is fantasy; but the same plot reappears in *The Great Gatsby,* where it is surrounded by the real world of the 1920s and for the first time it is carried through to its logical conclusion.

III

There is a moment in any real author's career when he suddenly becomes capable of doing his best work. He has found a fable that expresses his central truth and everything falls into place around it, so that his whole experience of life is available for use in his fiction. Something like that happened to Fitzgerald when he invented the story of Jimmy Gatz, otherwise known as Jay Gatsby, and it explains the amazing richness and scope of a very short novel.

To put facts on record, *The Great Gatsby* is a book of about fifty thousand words, a small structure built of nine chapters like big blocks. The fifth chapter—Gatsby's meeting with Daisy Buchanan—is the center of the narrative, as is proper; the seventh chapter is the climax. Each chapter consists of one or more dramatic scenes, sometimes with intervening passages of straight narration. The "scenic" method is one that Fitzgerald probably learned from Edith Wharton, who in turn learned it from Henry James; at any rate the book is technically in the Jamesian tradition (and Daisy Buchanan is named for James's heroine, Daisy Miller).

Part of the tradition is the device of having the story told by a single observer, who stands somewhat apart from the action and whose vision "frames" it for the reader. In this case the observer plays a special role. Although Nick Carraway doesn't save or ruin Gatsby, his personality in itself provides an essential comment on all the other characters. Nick stands for the older values that prevailed in the Middle West before the First World War. His family isn't tremendously rich, like the Buchanans, but it has a long established and sufficient fortune, so that Nick is the only person in the book who hasn't been corrupted by seeking or spending money. He is so certain of his own values that he hesitates to criticize others, but when he does pass judgment—on Gatsby, on Jordan Baker, on the Buchanans—he speaks as if for ages to come.

All the other characters belong to their own brief era of confused and dissolving standards, but they are affected by the era in different fashions. Each of them, we note on reading the book a second time, represents some particular variety of moral failure; Lionel Trilling says that they are "treated as if they were ideographs," a true observation; but the treatment does not detract from their reality as persons. Tom Buchanan is wealth brutalized by selfishness and arrogance; he looks for a mistress in the valley of ashes and finds an ignorant woman, Myrtle Wilson, whose raw vitality is like his own. Daisy Buchanan is the spirit of wealth and offers a continual promise "that she had done gay, exciting, things just a while since and that there were gay, exciting things hovering in the next hour"; but it is a false promise, since at heart she is as self-centered as Tom and even colder. Jordan Baker apparently lives by the old standards, but she uses them only as a subterfuge. Aware of her own cowardice and dishonesty, she feels "safer on a plane where any divergence from a code would be thought impossible."

All these, except Myrtle Wilson, are East Egg people, that is, they are part of a community where wealth takes the form of solid possessions. Set against them are the West Egg people, whose wealth is fluid income that might cease overnight. The West Egg people, with Gatsby as their archetype and tragic hero, have worked furiously to rise in the world, but they will never reach East Egg for all the money they spend; at most they can sit at the water's edge and look across the bay at the green light that shines and promises at the end of the Buchanans' dock. The symbolism of place has a great part in Fitzgerald's novel, as has that of motorcars. The characters are visibly represented by the cars they drive: Nick has a conservative old Dodge, the Buchanans, too rich for ostentation, have an "easy-going blue coupé," while Gatsby's car is "a rich cream color, bright with nickel, swollen here and there in its monstrous length with triumphant hat-boxes and supper-boxes and tool-boxes, and terraced with a labyrinth of wind-shields that mirrored a dozen suns"—it is West Egg on wheels. When Daisy drives through the valley of ashes in Gatsby's car, she causes the two deaths that end the story.

The symbols are not synthetic or contrived, like those in so many recent novels; they are images that Fitzgerald instinctively found to represent his characters and their destiny. When he says,

"Daisy took her face in her hands as if feeling its lovely shape," he is watching her act the charade of her self-love. When he says, "Tom would drift on forever seeking, a little wistfully, for the dramatic turbulence of some irrecoverable football game," he suggests the one appealing side of Tom's nature. He is so familiar with the characters and their background, so absorbed in their fate, that the book has an admirable unity of texture; we can open it to any page and find another of the touches that illuminate the story. We end by feeling that *Gatsby* has a double virtue. Except for *The Sun Also Rises* it is the best picture we possess of the age in which it was written and it also achieves a sort of moral permanence. Fitzgerald's story of the innocent murdered suitor for wealth is a compendious fable of the 1920s that will survive as a legend for other times.

FORD MADOX FORD ON

A *Farewell to Arms*
by Ernest Hemingway, 1929

As *founder and editor of* The Transatlantic Review, *Ford Madox Ford published the early work of many young experimental writers, among them Ezra Pound, James Joyce, and Ernest Hemingway. Before the demise of the* Review *in 1924, Hemingway served briefly on its editorial staff, an interlude that forms the background of this reminiscence and introduction to* A Farewell to Arms.

I experienced a singular sensation on reading the first sentence of *A Farewell to Arms*. There are sensations you cannot describe. You may know what causes them but you cannot tell what portions of your mind they affect nor yet, possibly, what parts of your physical entity. I can only say that it was as if I had found at last again something shining after a long delving amongst dust. I daresay prospectors after gold or diamonds feel something like that. But theirs can hardly be so coldly clear an emotion, or one so impersonal. The three impeccable writers of English prose that I have come across in fifty years or so of reading in search of English prose have been Joseph Conrad, W. H. Hudson . . . and Ernest Hemingway. . . . Impeccable each after his kind! I remember with equal clarity and equal indefinableness my sensation on first reading a sentence of each. With the Conrad it was like being overwhelmed by a great, unhastening wave. With the Hudson it was like lying on one's back and looking up into a clear, still sky. With the Hemingway it was just excitement. Like waiting at the side of a coppice, when foxhunting, for the hounds to break cover. One was going on a long chase in dry clear weather, one did not know in what direction or over what country.

Ernest Hemingway

The first sentence of Hemingway that I ever came across was not of course: "In the late summer of that year we lived in a house in a village that looked across the river and the plain towards the mountains." That is the opening of *Farewell to Arms*. No, my first sentence of Hemingway was:

"Everybody was drunk." *Tout court!* Like that!

Exactly how much my emotion gained from immediately afterwards reading the rest of the paragraph I can't say.

It runs for the next few sentences as follows:

> Everybody was drunk. The whole battery was drunk going along the road in the dark. We were going to the Champagne. The lieutenant kept riding his horse out into the fields and saying to him, "I'm drunk, I tell you, mon vieux. Oh, I am so soused." We went along the road in the dark and the adjutant kept riding up alongside my kitchen and saying, "You must put it out. It is dangerous. It will be observed."

I am reading from *"N° 3 of 170 hand-made copies printed on* rives *hand-made paper."* which is inscribed: "to robert mcalmon and william bird *publishers of the city of paris* and to captain edward dormansmith m.c., of *his majesty's fifth fusiliers* this book is respectfully dedicated." The title page, curiously enough bears the date 1924 but the copy is inscribed to me by Ernest Hemingway "march 1923" and must, as far as I can remember have been given to me then. There is a nice problem for bibliophiles.

This book is the first version of *In Our Time* and is described as published at "paris, *printed at* the three mountains press *and for sale at* shakespeare & company *in the rue de l'odéon; london:* william jackson, *took's court, cursitor street, chancery lane.*"

Those were the brave times in Paris when William Bird and I, and I daresay Hemingway too believed, I don't know why, that salvation could be found in leaving out capitals. We printed and published in a domed wine-vault, exceedingly old and cramped, on the Ile St. Louis with a grey view on the Seine below the Quais. It must have been salvation we aspired to for thoughts of fortune seldom came near us and Fortune herself, never. Publisher Bird printed his books beautifully at a great old seventeenth-century press and we all took hands at pulling its immense levers about. I "edited" in a gallery like a bird-cage at the top of the vault. It was so low that I could never stand up. Ezra also "edited" somewhere, I daresay, in the rue Notre Dame des Champs. At any rate the last page but one of *In Our Time*—or perhaps it is the *feuille de garde*, carries the announcement:

Here ends *The Inquest* into the state of
contemporary English prose, as
edited by EZRA POUND and printed at
the THREE MOUNTAINS PRESS. The six
works constituting the series are:
Indiscretions *of* Ezra Pound
Women and Men *by* Ford Madox Ford
Elimus *by* B. C. Windeler
with Designs *by* D. Shakespear
The Great American Novel
by William Carlos Williams
England *by* B. M. G. Adams
In Our Time *by* Ernest Hemingway
with portrait *by* Henry Strater.

Mr. Pound, you perceive did believe in Capitals and so obviously did one half of Hemingway for his other book of the same date— a blue-grey pamphlet—announces itself all in capitals of great baldness. (They are I believe of the style called *sans-sérif*):

THREE STORIES
& TEN POEMS
ERNEST HEMINGWAY

it calls itself without even a *'by'* in italics. There is no date or publisher's or distributor's name or address on the title page but the back of the half-title bears the small notices

Copyright 1923 by the author
Published by
Contact Publishing Co.

and the last page but one has the announcement

PRINTED AT DIJON
BY
MAURICE DARANTIERE
M.CX.XXIII

This copy bears an inscription in the handwriting of Mr. Hemingway to the effect that it was given to me in Paris by himself in 1924. That seems almost an exaggeration in antedating.

Anyhow, I read first *In Our Time* and then "My Old Man" in *Ten Stories* both in 1923. . . .

Those were exciting times in Paris. The Young-American literature that today forms the most important phase of the literary world anywhere was getting itself born there. And those were birth-throes!

Young America from the limitless prairies leapt, released, on Paris. They stampeded with the madness of colts when you let down the slip-rails between dried pasture and green. The noise of their advancing drowned all sounds. Their innumerable forms hid the very trees on the boulevards. Their perpetual motion made you dizzy. The falling plane-leaves that are the distinguishing mark of grey, quiet Paris, were crushed under foot and vanished like flakes of snow in tormented seas.

I might have been described as—by comparison—a nice, quiet gentleman for an elderly tea-party. And there I was between, as it were, the too quiet aestheticisms of William Bird, publisher supported by Ezra Pound, poet-editor, and, at the other extreme, Robert McAlmon damn-your-damn-highbrow-eyes author-publisher, backed by a whole Horde of Montparnasse from anywhere between North Dakota and Missouri. . . . You should have seen those Thursday tea-parties at the uncapitalled *Transatlantic Review* offices! The French speak of "la semaine à deux jeudis" . . . the week with two Thursdays in it. Mine seemed to contain sixty, judging by the noise, lung-power, crashing in, and denunciation. They sat on forms—school benches—cramped round Bird's great hand press. On the top of it was an iron eagle. A seventeenth-century eagle!

Where exactly between William Bird, hand-printer and publisher and Robert McAlmon, nine-hundred horse power linotype-publisher Hemingway came in I never quite found out. He was presented to me by Ezra and Bill Bird and had rather the aspect of an Eton-Oxford, husky-ish young captain of a midland regiment of His Britannic Majesty. In that capacity he entered the phalanxes of *The Transatlantic Review*. I forget what his official title was. He was perhaps joint-editor—or an advisory or consulting or vetoing editor. Of those there was a considerable company. I, I have omitted to say, was supposed to be Editor in Chief. They all shouted at me: I did not know how to write, or knew too much to be able to write, or did not know how to edit, or keep accounts, or sing *"Franky & Johnny,"* or order a dinner. The ceiling was vaulted, the plane-leaves drifted down on the quays outside; the grey Seine flowed softly.

Into the animated din would drift Hemingway, balancing on the point of his toes, feinting at my head with hands as large as hams and relating sinister stories of Paris landlords. He told them with singularly choice words in a slow voice. He still struck me as disciplined. Even captains of his majesty's fifth fusiliers are sometimes amateur pugilists and now and then dance on their toe-points in private. I noticed less however of Eton and Oxford. He seemed more a creature of wild adventures amongst steers in infinitudes.

All the same, when I went to New York, I confided that review to him. I gave him strict injunctions as to whom not to print and above all whom not to cut.

The last mortal enemy he made for me died yesterday. Hemingway had cut *his* article and all those of my most cherished and awful contributors down to a line or two apiece. In return he had printed all *his* wildest friends *in extenso*. So that uncapitalised review died. I don't say that it died of Hemingway. I still knew he must somehow be disciplined.

But, a day or two after my return, we were all lunching in the little bistro that was next to the office. There were a great many people and each of them was accusing me of some different incapacity. At last Hemingway extended an enormous seeming ham

under my nose. He shouted. What he shouted I could not hear but
I realised I had a pencil. Under the shadow of that vast and men-
acing object I wrote verses on the tablecloth.

> Heaven over-arches earth and sea
> Earth sadness and sea-hurricanes.
> Heaven over-arches you and me.
> A little while and we shall be
> Please God, where there is no more sea
> And no . . .

The reader may supply the rhyme.

That was the birth of a nation.

At any rate if America counts in the comity of civilised nations
it is by her new writers that she has achieved that immense feat.
So it seems to me. The reader trained in other schools of.thought
must bear with it. A nation exists by its laws, inventions, mass-
products. It lives for other nations by its arts.

I do not propose here to mention other names than those of
Ernest Hemingway. It is not my business to appraise. Appraise-
ments imply censures and it is not one writer's business to censure
others. A writer should expound other writers or let them alone.

When I thought that Hemingway had discipline I was not mistaken. He had then and still has the discipline that makes you avoid
temptation in the selection of words and the discipline that lets you
be remorselessly economical in the number that you employ. If, as
writer you have those disciplined knowledges or instincts, you may
prize fight or do what you like with the rest of your time.

The curse of English prose is that English words have double
effects. They have their literal meanings and then associations they
attain from other writers that have used them. These associations
as often as not come from the Authorised Version or the Book of
Common Prayer. You use a combination of words once used by
Archbishop Cranmer or Archbishop Warham or the Translators in
the XVI & XVII centuries. You expect to get from them an overtone
of awfulness, or erudition or romance or pomposity. So your prose
dies.

Hemingway's words strike you, each one, as if they were pebbles fetched fresh from a brook. They live and shine, each in its place. So one of his pages has the effect of a brook-bottom into which you look down through the flowing water. The words form a tessellation, each in order beside the other.

It is a very great quality. It is indeed the supreme quality of the written art of the moment. It is a great part of what makes literature come into its own at such rare times as it achieves that feat. Books lose their hold on you as soon as the words in which they are written are demoded or too usual the one following the other. The aim— the achievement—of the great prose writer is to use words so that they shall seem new and alive because of their juxtaposition with other words. This gift Hemingway has supremely. Any sentence of his taken at random will hold your attention. And irresistibly. It does not matter where you take it.

> I was in under the canvas with guns. They smelled cleanly of oil and grease. I lay and listened to the rain on the canvas and the clicking of the car over the rails. There was a little light came through and I lay and looked at the guns.

You could not begin that first sentence and not finish the passage. That is a great part of this author's gift. Yet it is not only "gift." You cannot throw yourself into a frame of mind and just write and get that effect. Your mind has to choose each word and your ear has to test it until by long disciplining of mind and ear you can no longer go wrong.

That disciplining through which you must put yourself is all the more difficult in that it must be gone through in solitude. You cannot watch the man next to you in the ranks smartly manipulating his side-arms nor do you hear any word of command by which to time yourself.

On the other hand a writer holds a reader by his temperament. That is his true "gift"—what he receives from whoever sends him into the world. It arises from how you look at things. If you look at and render things so that they appear new to the reader you will hold his attention. If what you give him appears familiar or half familiar his attention will wander. Hemingway's use of the word "cleanly" is an instance of what I have just been saying. The guns smelled cleanly of oil and grease. Oil and grease are not usually associated in the mind with a clean smell. Yet at the minutest reflection you realise that the oil and grease on the clean metal of big guns are not dirt. So the adverb is just. You have had a moment of surprise and then your knowledge is added to. The word "author" means "someone who adds to your consciousness."

When, in those old days, Hemingway used to tell stories of his Paris landlords he used to be hesitant, to pause between words and then to speak gently but with great decision. His temperament was selecting the instances he should narrate, his mind selecting the words to employ. The impression was one of a person using restraint at the biddings of discipline. It was the right impression to have had.

He maintains his hold on himself up to the last word of every unit of his prose. The last words of "My Old Man" are:

> But I don't know. Seems like when they get started they don't leave a guy nothing.

The last words of *In Our Time*:

> It was very jolly. We talked for a long time. Like all Greeks he wanted to go to America.

A *Farewell to Arms* ends incomparably:

> But after I had got them out and shut the door and turned out the light it wasn't any good. It was like saying good-by to a statue. After a while I went out and left the hospital and walked back to the hotel in the rain.

Incomparably, because that muted passage after great emotion still holds the mind after the book is finished. The interest prolongs itself and the reader is left wishing to read more of that writer's.

After the first triumphant success of a writer a certain tremulousness besets his supporters in the public. It is the second book that is going to have a rough crossing. . . . Or the third and the fourth. So after the great artistic triumph of William Bird's edition of *In Our Time* Hemingway seemed to me to falter. He produced a couple of books that I did not much like. I was probably expected not much to like them. Let us say that they were essays towards a longer form than that of the episodic *In Our Time*. Then with *Men Without Women* he proved that he retained the essential gift. In that volume there is an episodic-narrative that moves you as you will—if you are to be moved at all—be moved by episodes of the Greek Anthology. It has the same quality of serene flawlessness.

In the last paragraph I have explained the nature of my emotion when I read a year or so ago that first sentence of *Farewell to Arms*. It was more than excitement. It was excitement plus re-assurance. The sentence was exactly the right opening for a long piece of work. To read it was like looking at an athlete setting out on a difficult and prolonged effort. You say, at the first movement of the limbs: "It's all right. He's in form. . . . He'll do today what he has never quite done before." And you settle luxuriantly into your seat.

So I read on after the first sentence:

> In the bed of the river there were pebbles and boulders dry and white in the sun, and the water was clear and swiftly moving and blue in the channels. Troops went by the house and down the road and the dust they raised powdered the leaves of the trees. The trunks of the trees were dusty and the leaves fell early that year and we saw the troops marching along the road and the dust rising and the leaves, stirred by the breeze falling and the soldiers marching and afterwards the road bare and white except for the leaves.

I wish I could quote more, it is such pleasure to see words like that come from one's pen. But you can read it for yourself.

A Farewell to Arms is a book important in the annals of the art of writing because it proves that Hemingway, the writer of short, perfect episodes, can keep up the pace through a volume. There have been other writers of impeccable—of matchless—prose but as a rule their sustained efforts have palled because precisely of the remarkableness of the prose itself. You can hardly read *Marius the Epicurean*. You may applaud its author, Walter Pater. But *A Farewell to Arms* is without purple patches or even verbal "felicities." Whilst you are reading it you forget to applaud its author. You do not know that you are having to do with an author. You are living.

Ernest Hemingway

A *Farewell to Arms* is a book that unites the critic to the simple. You could read it and be thrilled if you had never read a book—or if you had read and measured all the good books in the world. That is the real province of the art of writing.

Hemingway has other fields to conquer. That is no censure on A *Farewell to Arms*. It is not blaming the United States to say that she has not yet annexed Nicaragua. But whatever he does can never take away from the fresh radiance of this work. It may close with tears but it is like a spring morning.

MAXWELL E. PERKINS ON

Look Homeward, Angel
by Thomas Wolfe, 1929

This introduction, originally intended for the Wolfe collection at the Harvard College Library and later adopted for the 1957 edition of Look Homeward, Angel, *tells the story of editor Maxwell Perkins's professional and personal relationship with Wolfe. Perkins was working on it when he died in 1947.*

I think that there is not in any one place so nearly complete a collection of an author's writings and records as that of Thomas Wolfe's now in the Harvard Library When he died on that sad day in September 1938, when war wa impending, or soon after that, I learned that I was his executo and that he had actually left little—as he would have thought, and as it seemed then—besides his manuscripts. It was my obligatio to dispose of them to the advantage of his beneficiaries and hi memory, and though the times were bad, and Wolfe had not the been recognized as what he now is, I could have sold them com mercially, piecemeal, through dealers, for more money than the ever brought. I was determined that this literary estate shoul remain a unit, available to writers and students, and I tried to sel it as such; but at that time, with war clouds gathering and soo bursting, I could find no adequate buyer.

Then Aline Bernstein, to whom Wolfe had given the manuscrip of *Look Homeward, Angel,* sold it by auction for the relief of he people in misfortune, on the understanding that it would be give to Harvard. Not long after that William B. Wisdom, who had rec ognized Wolfe as a writer of genius on the publication of the *Angel* and whose faith in him had never wavered, offered to purchase al

of his manuscripts and records. He had already accumulated a
notable collection of Wolfiana. His correspondence showed me that
he thought as I did—that the point of supreme importance was
that these records and writings should not be scattered to the
four winds, that they be kept intact. And so the whole great packing case of material—letters, bills, documents, notebooks and
manuscripts—went to him on the stipulation, which I never need
have asked for, that he would will it all to one institution. Since
Look Homeward, Angel was already in Harvard, since Tom Wolfe
had loved the reading room of the Library where, as he so often
told me, he devoured his hundreds of books and spent most of his
Harvard years, Mr. Wisdom made a gift of all this to Harvard. And
there it now is.

Though I had worked as an editor with Thomas Wolfe on two
huge manuscripts, *Look Homeward, Angel* and *Of Time and the River*,
I was astonished on that Spring evening of 1935 when Tom, about
to sail for England, brought to our house on East 49th Street,
because Scribner's was closed, the huge packing case containing all
his literary material. Tom and I and the taxi man carried it in and
set it down. Then Tom said to the man, "What is your name?" He
said, "Lucky." "Lucky!" said Tom—I think it was perhaps an Amer-
icanization of some Italian name—and grasped his hand. It seemed
a good omen. We three had done something together. We were
together for that moment. We all shook hands. But for days, that
huge packing case blocked our hall, until I got it removed to Scribner's.

The first time I heard of Thomas Wolfe I had a sense of fore-
boding. I who love the man say this. Every good thing that comes
is accompanied by trouble. It was in 1928 when Madeleine Boyd,
a literary agent, came in. She talked of several manuscripts which
did not much interest me, but frequently interrupted herself to tell
of a wonderful novel about an American boy. I several times said
to her, "Why don't you bring it in here, Madeleine?" and she seemed
to evade the question. But finally she said, "I will bring it, if you
promise to read every word of it." I did promise, but she told me
other things that made me realize that Wolfe was a turbulent spirit,
and that we were in for turbulence. When the manuscript came,

I was fascinated by the first scene where Eugene's father, Oliver W. Gant, with his brother, two little boys, stood by a roadside in Pennsylvania and saw a division of Lee's Army on the march to Gettysburg.

But then there came some ninety-odd pages about Oliver Gant's life in Newport News, and Baltimore, and elsewhere. All this was what Wolfe had heard, and had no actual association with which to reconcile it, and it was inferior to the first episode, and in fact to all the rest of the book. I was turned off to other work and gave the manuscript to Wallace Meyer, thinking, "Here is another promising novel that probably will come to nothing." Then Meyer showed me that wonderful night scene in the café where Ben was with the Doctors, and Horse Hines, the undertaker, came in. I dropped everything and began to read again, and all of us were reading the book simultaneously, you might say, including John Hall Wheelock, and there never was the slightest disagreement among us as to its importance.

After some correspondence between me and Wolfe, and between him and Madeleine Boyd, from which we learned how at the October Fair in Germany he had been almost beaten to death—when I realized again that we had a Moby-Dick to deal with—Wolfe arrived in New York and stood in the doorway of my boxstall of an office leaning against the door jamb. When I looked up and saw his wild hair and bright countenance—although he was so altogether different physically—I thought of Shelley. *He* was fair, but his hair was wild, and his face was bright and his head disproportionately small.

We then began to work upon the book and the first thing we did, to give it unity, was to cut out that wonderful scene it began with and the ninety-odd pages that followed, because it seemed to me, and he agreed, that the whole tale should be unfolded through the memories and senses of the boy, Eugene, who was born in Asheville. We both thought that the story was compassed by that child's realization; that it was life and the world as he came to realize them. When he had tried to go back into the life of his father before he arrived in Asheville, without the inherent memory of events, the reality and the poignance were diminished—but for years it was on my conscience that I had persuaded Tom to cut out that first scene of the two little boys on the roadside with Gettysburg impending.

And then what happened? In *Of Time and the River* he brought the scene back to greater effect when old Gant was dying on the gallery of the hospital in Baltimore and in memory recalled his olden days. After that occurred I felt much less anxiety in suggesting cuts: I began then to realize that nothing Wolfe wrote was ever lost, that omissions from one book were restored in a later one. An extreme example of this is the fact that the whole second half of *The Web and the Rock* was originally intended to be the concluding episode in *Of Time and the River*. But most, and perhaps almost all, of those early incidents of Gant's life were worked into *The Web and the Rock* and *You Can't Go Home Again*.

I had realized, for Tom had prefaced his manuscript with a statement to that effect, that *Look Homeward, Angel* was autobiographical, but I had come to think of it as being so in the sense that *David Copperfield* is, or *War and Peace*, or *Pendennis*. But when we were working together, I suddenly saw that it was often almost literally autobiographical—that these people in it were his people. I am sure my face took on a look of alarm, and Tom saw it and he said, "But Mr. Perkins, you don't understand. I think these people are *great* people and that they should be told about." He was right. He had written a great book, and it had to be taken substantially as it was. And in truth, the extent of cutting in that book has somehow come to be greatly exaggerated. Really, it was more a matter of reorganization. For instance, Tom had that wonderful episode when Gant came back from his far-wandering and rode in early morning on the trolley car through the town and heard about who had died and who had been born and saw all the scenes that were so familiar to Tom or Eugene, as the old trolley rumbled along. This was immediately followed by an episode of a similar kind where Eugene, with his friends, walked home from school through the town of Asheville. That was presented in a Joycean way, but it was the same sort of thing—some one going through the town and through his perceptions revealing it to the reader. By putting these episodes next to each other the effect of each was diminished, and I think we gave both much greater value by separating them. We did a great deal of detailed cutting, but it was such things as that I speak of that constituted perhaps the greater part of the work.

Of Time and the River was a much greater struggle for Tom. Eventually, I think it was on Thanksgiving Day 1933, he brought me in desperation about two feet of typescript. The first scene in this was the platform of the railroad station in Asheville when Eugene was about to set out for Harvard, and his family had come to see him off. It must have run to about 30,000 words and I cut it to perhaps 10,000 and showed it to Tom. He approved it. When you are waiting for a train to come in, there is suspense. Something is going to happen. You must, it seemed to me, maintain that sense of suspense and you can't to the extent of 30,000 words. There never was any cutting that Tom did not agree to. He knew that cutting was necessary. His whole impulse was to utter what he felt and he had no time to revise and compress.

So then we began a year of nights of work, including Sundays, and every cut, and change, and interpolation, was argued about and about. The principle that I was working on was that this book, too, got its unity and its form through the senses of Eugene, and I remember how, if I had had my way, we should, by sticking to that principle, have lost one of the most wonderful episodes Wolfe ever wrote—the death of Gant. One night we agreed that certain transitions should be written in, but instead of doing them Wolfe brought on the next night some 5,000 words about Eugene's sister in Asheville when her father was ill, and a doctor there and a nurse. I said, "Tom, this is all outside the story, and you know it. Eugene was not there, he was in Cambridge; all of this was outside his perception and knowledge at the time." Tom agreed with me, but the next night, he brought me another 5,000 words or so which got up into the death of Gant. And then I realized I was wrong, even if right in theory. What he was doing was too good to let any rule of form impede him.

It is said that Tolstoy never willingly parted with the manuscript of *War and Peace*. One could imagine him working on it all through his life. Certainly Thomas Wolfe never willingly parted from the proofs of *Of Time and the River*. He sat brooding over them for weeks in the Scribner library and not reading. John Wheelock read them and we sent them to the printer and told Tom it had been done. I could believe that otherwise he might have clung to them to the end.

He dedicated that book to me in most extravagant terms. I never saw the dedication until the book was published and though I was most grateful for it, I had forebodings when I heard of his intention. I think it was that dedication that threw him off his stride and broke his magnificent scheme. It gave shallow people the impression that Wolfe could not function as a writer without collaboration, and one critic even used some such phrases as, "Wolfe and Perkins—Perkins and Wolfe, what way is that to write a novel." Nobody with the slightest comprehension of the nature of a writer could accept such an assumption. No writer could possibly tolerate the assumption, which perhaps Tom almost himself did, that he was dependent as a writer upon anyone else. He had to prove to himself and to the world that this was not so.

And that was the fundamental reason that he turned to another publisher. If he had not—but by the time he did it was plain that he had to tell, in the medium of fiction and through the trans-mutation of his amazing imagination, the story of his own life—he never would have broken his own great plan by distorting Eugene Gant into George Webber. That was a horrible mistake. I think Edward Aswell, of Harper & Brothers, agrees with me in this, but when the manuscript that came to form *The Web and the Rock* and *You Can't Go Home Again* got to him to work on, and in some degree to me, as Wolfe's executor, Tom was dead, and things had to be taken as they were.

The trouble began after the publication of *Of Time and the River*, which the reviewers enormously praised—but many of them as-serted that Wolfe could only write about himself, that he could not see the world or anything objectively, with detachment—that he was always autobiographical. Wolfe was extremely sensitive to criticism, for all his tremendous faith in his genius as an obligation put upon him to fulfill. One day when I lived on East 49th Street near Second Avenue, and he on First Avenue, just off the corner of 49th, I met him as I was going home. He said he wanted to talk to me, as we did talk every evening about that time, and we went into the Waldorf. He referred to the criticisms against him, and said that he wanted to write a completely objective, unautobiographical book, and that it would show how strangely different everything is from what a person expects it to be. One might say that he was thinking of the theme that has run through so many great books, such as *Pickwick Papers* and *Don Quixote*, where a man, young or old, goes hopefully out into the world slap into the face of outrageous reality. He was going to put on the title page what was said by Prince Andrei, in *War and Peace*, after his first battle, when the praise fell upon those who had done nothing and blame almost fell upon one who had done everything. Prince Andrei, who saved the battery commander who most of all had held back the French from the blame that Little Tushin would have accepted, walked out with him into the night. Then as Tushin left, Tolstoy said, "Prince Andrei looked up at the stars and sighed; everything was so different from what he thought it was going to be."

Tom was in a desperate state. It was not only what the critics said that made him wish to write objectively, but that he knew that what he had written had given great pain even to those he loved the most. The conclusion of our talk was that if he could write such an objective book on this theme within a year, say, to the extent of perhaps a hundred thousand words, it might be well to do it. It was this that turned him to George Webber, but once he began on that he really and irresistibly resumed the one story he was destined to write, which was that of himself, or Eugene Gant.

And so, the first half of *The Web and the Rock*, of which there is only a typescript, is a re-telling in different terms of *Look Homeward, Angel*. Wolfe was diverted from his natural purpose—and even had he lived, what could have been done? Some of his finest writing is that first half of *The Web and the Rock*. Could anybody have just tossed it out?

But if Tom had held to his scheme and completed the whole story of his life as transmuted into fiction through his imagination, I think the accusation that he had no sense of form could not have stood. He wrote one long story, "The Web of Earth," which had perfect form, for all its intricacy. I remember saying to him, "Not one word of this should be changed." One might say that as his own physical dimensions were huge so was his conception of a book. He had one book to write about a vast, sprawling, turbulent land —America—as perceived by Eugene Gant. Even when he was in Europe, it was of America he thought. If he had not been diverted and had lived to complete it, I think it would have had the form that was suited to the subject.

His detractors say he could only write about himself, but all that he wrote of was transformed by his imagination. For instance, in *You Can't Go Home Again* he shows the character Foxhall Edwards at breakfast. Edwards's young daughter enters "as swiftly and silently as a ray of light." She is very shy and in a hurry to get to school. She tells of a theme she has written on Walt Whitman and what the teacher said of Whitman. When Edwards urges her not to hurry and makes various observations, she says, "Oh, Daddy, you're so funny!" What Tom did was to make one unforgettable little character out of three daughters of Foxhall Edwards.

He got the ray of light many years ago when he was with me in my house in New Canaan, Connecticut, and one daughter, at the age of about eight or ten, came in and met this gigantic stranger. After she was introduced she fluttered all about the room in her embarrassment, but radiant, like a sunbeam. Then Tom was present when another daughter, in Radcliffe, consulted me about a paper she was writing on Whitman, but he put this back into her school days. The third, of which he composed a single character, was the youngest, who often did say, partly perhaps, because she was not at ease when Tom was there, "Oh, Daddy, you're so silly." That is how Tom worked. He created something new and something meaningful through a transmutation of what he saw, heard, and realized.

I think no one could understand Thomas Wolfe who had not

seen or properly imagined the place in which he was born and grew up. Asheville, North Carolina, is encircled by mountains. The trains wind in and out through labyrinths of passes. A boy of Wolfe's imagination imprisoned there could think that what was beyond was all wonderful—different from what it was where there was not for him enough of anything. Whatever happened, Wolfe would have been what he was. I remember on the day of his death saying to his sister Mabel that I thought it amazing in an American family that one of the sons who wanted to be a writer should have been given the support that was given Tom, and that they all deserved great credit for that. She said it didn't matter, that nothing could have prevented Tom from doing what he did.

That is true, but I think that those mountainous walls which his imagination vaulted gave him the vision of an America with which his books are fundamentally concerned. He often spoke of the artist in America—how the whole color and character of the country was completely new—never interpreted; how in England, for instance, the writer inherited a long accretion of accepted expression from which he could start. But Tom would say—and he had seen the world—"who has ever made you know the color of an American box car?" Wolfe was in those mountains—he tells of the train whistles at night—the trains were winding their way out into the great world where it seemed to the boy there was everything desirable, and vast, and wonderful.

It was partly that which made him want to see everything, and read everything, and experience everything, and say everything. There was a night when he lived on First Avenue that Nancy Hale, who lived on East 49th Street near Third Avenue, heard a kind of chant, which grew louder. She got up and looked out of the window at two or three in the morning and there was the great figure of Thomas Wolfe, advancing in his long countryman's stride, with his swaying black raincoat, and what he was chanting was, "I wrote ten thousand words today—I wrote ten thousand words today."

Tom must have lived in eight or nine different parts of New York and Brooklyn for a year or more. He knew in the end every aspect of the City—he walked the streets endlessly—but he was not a city man. The city fascinated him but he did not really belong in it and was never satisfied to live in it. He was always thinking of America as a whole and planning trips to some part that he had not yet seen, and in the end taking them. His various quarters in town always looked as if he had just moved in, to camp for awhile. This was partly because he really had no interest in possessions of any kind, but it was also because he was in his very nature a Far Wanderer, bent upon seeing all places, and his rooms were just necessities into which he never settled. Even when he was there his mind was not. He needed a continent to range over, actually and in imagination. And his place was all America. It was with America he was most deeply concerned and I believe he opened it up as no other writer ever did for the people of his time and for the writers and artists and poets of tomorrow. Surely he had a thing to tell us.

Sanctuary
by William Faulkner, 1931

Sanctuary, *written for money, was the first novel that earned Faulkner both critical and popular acclaim. Bennett Cerf at Random House wanted it for The Modern Library series and convinced Faulkner to write this now famous introduction for that edition.*

This book was written three years ago. To me it is a cheap idea, because it was deliberately conceived to make money. I had been writing books for about five years, which got published and not bought. But that was all right. I was young then and hard-bellied. I had never lived among nor known people who wrote novels and stories and I suppose I did not know that people got money for them. I was not very much annoyed when publishers refused the mss. now and then. Because I was hard-gutted then, I could do a lot of things that could earn what little money I needed, thanks to my father's unfailing kindness which supplied me with bread at need despite the outrage to his principles at having been of a bum progenitive.

Then I began to get a little soft. I could still paint houses and do carpenter work, but I got soft. I began to think about making money by writing. I began to be concerned when magazine editors turned down short stories, concerned enough to tell them that they would buy these stories later anyway, and hence why not now. Meanwhile, with one novel completed and consistently refused for two years, I had just written my guts into *The Sound and the Fury* though I was not aware until the book was published that I had done so, because I had done it for pleasure. I believed then that I would never be published again. I had stopped thinking of myself in publishing terms.

William Faulkner

But when the third mss., *Sartoris,* was taken by a publisher and (he having refused *The Sound and the Fury*) it was taken by still another publisher, who warned me at the time that it would not sell, I began to think of myself again as a printed object. I began to think of books in terms of possible money. I decided I might just as well make some of it myself. I took a little time out, and speculated what a person in Mississippi would believe to be current trends, chose what I thought was the right answer and invented the most horrific tale I could imagine and wrote it in about three weeks and sent it to Smith, who had done *The Sound and the Fury* and who wrote me immediately, "Good God, I can't publish this. We'd both be in jail." So I told Faulkner, "You're damned. You'll have to work now and then for the rest of your life." That was in the summer of 1929. I got a job in the power plant, on the night shift, from 6 P.M. to 6 A.M., as a coal passer. I shoveled coal from the bunker into a wheelbarrow and wheeled it in and dumped it where the fireman could put it into the boiler. About 11 o'clock the people would be going to bed, and so it did not take so much steam. Then we could rest, the fireman and I. He would sit in a chair and doze. I had invented a table out of a wheelbarrow in the coal bunker, just beyond a wall from where a dynamo ran. It made a deep, constant humming noise. There was no more work to do until about 4 A.M., when we would have to clean the fires and get up steam again. On these nights, between 12 and 4, I wrote *As I Lay Dying* in six weeks, without changing a word. I sent it to Smith and wrote him that by it I would stand or fall.

I think I had forgotten about *Sanctuary,* just as you might forget about anything made for an immediate purpose, which did not come off. *As I Lay Dying* was published and I didn't remember the mss. of *Sanctuary* until Smith sent me the galleys. Then I saw that it was so terrible that there were but two things to do: tear it up or rewrite it. I thought again, "It might sell; maybe 10,000 of them will buy it." So I tore the galleys down and rewrote the book. It had been already set up once, so I had to pay for the privilege of rewriting it, trying to make out of it something which would not shame *The Sound and the Fury* and *As I Lay Dying* too much and I made a fair job and I hope you will buy it and tell your friends and I hope they will buy it too.

JEAN-PAUL SARTRE ON

1919
by John Dos Passos, 1932

The work of Dos Passos served as a technical revelation to philosopher and novelist Jean-Paul Sartre, who was introducing it to his students in Le Havre even before it was translated into French. In this 1938 essay, he analyzes his admiration for 1919 and declares Dos Passos to be "the greatest writer of our time."

A novel is a mirror. So everyone says. But what is meant by *reading* a novel? It means, I think, jumping into the mirror. You suddenly find yourself on the other side of the glass, among people and objects that have a familiar look. But they merely look familiar. We have never really seen them. The things of our world have, in turn, become outside reflections. You close the book, step over the edge of the mirror and return to this honest-to-goodness world, and you find furniture, gardens and people who have nothing to say to you. The mirror that closed behind you reflects them peacefully, and now you would swear that art is a reflection. There are clever people who go so far as to talk of distorting mirrors.

Dos Passos very consciously uses this absurd and insistent illusion to impel us to revolt. He has done everything possible to make his novel seem a mere reflection. He has even donned the garb of populism. The reason is that his art is not gratuitous; he wants to prove something. But observe what a curious aim he has. He wants to show us this world, our own—to *show* it only, without explanations or comment. There are no revelations about the machinations of the police, the imperialism of the oil kings or the Ku-Klux-Klan, no cruel pictures of poverty. We have already seen everything he wants to show us, and, so it seems at first glance, seen it exactly as he wants us to see it. We recognize immediately the sad abundance of these untragic lives. They are our own lives, these innumerable, planned, botched, immediately forgotten and constantly renewed adventures that slip by without leaving a trace, without involving anyone, until the time when one of them, no different from any of the others, suddenly, as if through some clumsy trickery, sickens a man for good and throws a mechanism out of gear.

Now, it is by depicting, as we ourselves might depict, these too familiar appearances with which we all put up that Dos Passos makes them unbearable. He arouses indignation in people who never get indignant, he frightens people who fear nothing. But hasn't there been some sleight-of-hand? I look about me and see people, cities, boats, the war. But they aren't the real thing; they are discreetly queer and sinister, as in a nightmare. My indignation against this world also seems dubious to me; it only faintly resembles the other indignation, the kind that a mere news item can arouse. I am on the other side of the mirror.

Dos Passos' hate, despair and lofty contempt are real. But that is precisely why his world is not real; it is a created object. I know of none—not even Faulkner's or Kafka's—in which the art is greater or better hidden. I know of none that is more precious, more touching or closer to us. This is because he takes his material from our world. And yet, there is no stranger or more distant world. Dos Passos has invented only one thing, an art of story-telling. But that is enough to create a universe.

We live in time, we calculate in time. The novel, like life, unfolds in the present. The perfect tense exists on the surface only; it must be interpreted as a present *with aesthetic distance,* as a stage device. In the novel the dice are not loaded, for fictional man is free. He develops before our eyes; our impatience, our ignorance, our expectancy are the same as the hero's. The tale, on the other hand, as Fernandez has shown, develops in the past. But the tale explains. Chronological order, life's order, barely conceals the causal order, which is an order for the understanding. The event does not touch us; it stands half-way between fact and law. Dos Passos' time is his own creation; it is neither fictional nor narrative. It is rather, if you like, historical time. The perfect and imperfect tenses are not used simply to observe the rules; the reality of Joe's or of Eveline's adventures lies in the fact they are now part of the past. Everything is told as if by someone who is remembering.

> *"The years Dick was little* he never heard anything about his Dad. . . ." "All Eveline thought about *that winter* was going to the Art Institute. . . ." "They waited two weeks in Vigo while the officials quarrelled about their status and they got pretty fed up with it."

The fictional event is a nameless presence; there is nothing one can say about it, for it develops. We may be shown two men combing a city for their mistresses, but we are not told that they "do not find them," for this is not true. So long as there remains one street, one café, one house to explore, it is not yet true. In Dos Passos, the things that happen are named first, and then the dice are cast, as they are in our memories.

> Glen and Joe only got ashore for a few hours and couldn't find Marcelline and Loulou.

The facts are clearly outlined; they are ready for *thinking about*. But Dos Passos never thinks them. Not for an instant does the order of causality betray itself in chronological order. There is no narrative, but rather the jerky unreeling of a rough and uneven memory, which sums up a period of several years in a few words only to dwell languidly over a minute fact. Like our real memories, it is a jumble of miniatures and frescoes. There is relief enough, but it is cunningly scattered at random. One step further would give us the famous idiot's monologue in *The Sound and the Fury*. But that would still involve intellectualizing, suggesting an explanation in terms of the irrational, suggesting a Freudian order beneath this disorder. Dos Passos stops just in time. As a result of this, past things retain a flavour of the present; they still remain, in their exile, what they once were, inexplicable tumults of colour, sound and passion. Each event is irreducible, a gleaming and solitary *thing* that does not flow from anything else, but suddenly arises to join other things. For Dos Passos, narrating means adding. This accounts for the slack air of his style. "And . . . and . . . and . . ." The great disturbing phenomena—war, love, political movements, strikes—fade and crumble into an infinity of little odds and ends which can just about be set side by side. Here is the armistice:

> In early November rumours of an armistice began to fly around and then suddenly one afternoon Major Wood ran into the office that Eleanor and Eveline shared and dragged them both away from their desks and kissed them both and shouted, "At last it's come." Before she knew it Eveline found herself kissing Major Moorehouse right on the mouth. The Red Cross office turned into a college dormitory the night of a football victory: it was the Armistice.
>
> Everybody seemed suddenly to have bottles of cognac and to be singing, *There's a long trail awinding* or *La Madel-lon pour nous n'est pas sévère.*

These Americans see war the way Fabrizio saw the battle of Waterloo. And the intention, like the method, is clear upon reflection. But you must close the book and reflect.

Passions and gestures are also things. Proust analysed them, related them to former states and thereby made them inevitable. Dos Passos wants to retain only their factual nature. All he is allowed to say is, "In that place and at that time Richard was that way, and at another time, he was different." Love and decisions are great spheres that rotate on their own axes. The most we can grasp is a kind of *conformity* between the psychological state and the exterior situation, something resembling a colour harmony. We may also suspect that explanations are *possible*, but they seem as frivolous and futile as a spider-web on a heavy red flower. Yet, never do we have the feeling of fictional freedom: Dos Passos imposes upon us instead the unpleasant impression of an indeterminacy of detail. Acts, emotions and ideas suddenly settle within a character, make themselves at home and then disappear without his having much to say in the matter. You cannot say he submits to them. He experiences them. There seems to be no law governing their appearance.

Nevertheless, they once did exist. This lawless past is irremediable. Dos Passos has purposely chosen the perspective of history to tell a story. He wants to make us feel that the stakes are down. In *Man's Hope*, Malraux says, more or less, that "the tragic thing about death is that it transforms life into a destiny." With the opening lines of his book, Dos Passos settles down into death. The lives he tells about are all closed in on themselves. They resemble those Bergsonian memories which, after the body's death, float about, lifeless and full of odours and lights and cries, through some forgotten limbo. We constantly have the feeling that these vague, human lives are destinies. Our own past is not at all like this. There is not one of our acts whose meaning and value we cannot still transform even now. But beneath the violent colours of these beautiful, motley objects that Dos Passos presents there is something petrified. Their significance is fixed. Close your eyes and try to remember your own life, try to remember it *that way;* you will stifle. It is this unrelieved stifling that Dos Passos wanted to express. In capitalist society, men do not have lives, they have only destinies. He never says this, but he makes it felt throughout. He expresses it discreetly, cautiously, until we feel like smashing our destinies. We have become rebels; he has achieved his purpose.

We are rebels *behind the looking-glass.* For that is not what the rebel of this world wants to change. He wants to transform Man's *present* condition, the one that develops day by day. Using the past tense to tell about the present means using a device, creating a strange and beautiful world, as frozen as one of those Mardi-Gras masks that become frightening on the faces of real, living men.

But whose memories are these that unfold through the novel? At first glance, they seem to be those of the heroes, of Joe, Dick, Fillette and Eveline. And, on occasion, they are. As a rule, whenever a character is sincere, whenever he is bursting with something, no matter how, or with what:

> When he went off duty he'd walk home achingly tired through the strawberry-scented early Parisian morning, thinking of the faces and the eyes and the sweat-drenched hair and the clenched fingers clotted with blood and dirt . . .

But the narrator often ceases to coincide completely with the hero. The hero could not quite have said what he does say, but you feel a discreet complicity between them. The narrator relates from the outside what the hero would have wanted him to relate. By means of this complicity, Dos Passos, without warning us, has us make the transition he was after. We suddenly find ourselves inside a horrible memory whose every recollection makes us uneasy, a bewildering memory that is no longer that of either the characters or the author. It seems like a chorus that remembers, a sententious chorus that is accessory to the deed.

> All the same he got along very well at school and the teachers liked him, particularly Miss Teazle, the English teacher, because he had nice manners and said little things that weren't fresh but that made them laugh. Miss Teazle said he showed real feeling for English composition. One Christmas he sent her a little rhyme he made up about the Christ Child and the three Kings and she declared he had a gift.

The narration takes on a slightly stilted manner, and everything that is reported about the hero assumes the solemn quality of a public announcement: ". . . she declared he had a gift." The sentence is not accompanied by any comment, but acquires a sort of collective resonance. It is a *declaration*. And indeed, whenever we want to know his characters' thoughts, Dos Passos, with respectful objectivity, generally gives us their declarations.

> Fred . . . said the last night before they left he was going to tear loose. When they got to the front he might get killed and then what? Dick said he liked talking to the girls but that the whole business was too commercial and turned his stomach. Ed Schuyler, who'd been nicknamed Frenchie and was getting very continental in his ways, said that the street girls were too naive.

I open *Paris-Soir* and read, "*From our special correspondent*: Charlie Chaplin declares that he has put an end to Charlie." Now I have it! Dos Passos reports all his characters' utterances to us in the style of a statement to the Press. Their words are thereby cut off from thought, and become pure utterances, simple reactions that must be registered as such, in the behaviourist style upon which

Dos Passos draws when it suits him to do so. But, at the same time, the utterance takes on a social importance; it is inviolable, it becomes a maxim. Little does it matter, thinks the satisfied chorus, what Dick had in mind when he spoke that sentence. What matters is that it has been uttered. Besides, it was not formed inside him, it came from afar. Even before he uttered it, it existed as a pompous sound, a taboo. All he has done is to lend it his power of affirmation. It is as if there were a Platonic heaven of words and commonplaces to which we all go to find words suitable to a given situation. There is a heaven of gestures, too. Dos Passos makes a pretence of presenting gestures as pure events, as mere exteriors, as free, animal movements. But this is only appearance. Actually, in relating them, he adopts the point of view of the chorus, of public opinion. There is no single one of Dick's or of Eleanor's gestures which is not a public demonstration, performed to a humming accompaniment of flattery.

> At Chantilly they went through the château and fed the big carp in the moat. They ate their lunch in the woods, sitting on rubber cushions. J.W. kept everybody laughing explaining how he hated picnics, asking everybody what it was that got into even the most intelligent women that they were always trying to make people go on picnics. After lunch they drove out to Senlis to see the houses that the Uhlans had destroyed there in the battle of the Marne.

Doesn't it sound like a local newspaper's account of an exservicemen's banquet? All of a sudden, as the gesture dwindles until it is no more than a thin film, we see that it *counts*, that it is sacred in character and that, at the same time, it involves commitment. But for whom? For the abject consciousness of "everyman," for what Heidegger calls "das Mann." But still, where does it spring from? Who is its representative as I read? *I* am. In order to understand the words, in order to make sense out of the paragraphs, I first have to adopt his point of view. I have to play the role of the obliging chorus. This consciousness exists only through me; without me there would be nothing but black spots on white paper. But even while I *am* this collective consciousness, I want to wrench away from it, to see it from the judge's point of view, that is, to get free of myself. This is the source of the shame and uneasiness with which Dos Passos knows how to fill the reader. I am a reluctant accomplice (though I am not even sure that I am reluctant), creating and rejecting social taboos. I am, deep in my heart, a revolutionary again, an unwilling one.

In return, how I hate Dos Passos' men! I am given a fleeting glimpse of their minds, just enough to see that they are living animals. Then, they begin to unwind their endless tissue of ritual statements and sacred gestures. For them, there is no break between inside and outside, between body and consciousness, but only between the stammerings of an individual's timid, intermittent, fumbling thinking and the messy world of collective representations. What a simple process this is, and how effective! All one need do is use American journalistic technique in telling the story of a life, and like the Salzburg reed, a life crystallizes into the Social, and the problem of the transition to the typical—stumbling-block of the social novel—is thereby resolved. There is no further need to present a working man type, to compose (as Nizan does in *Antoine Bloyé*) an existence which represents the exact average of thousands of existences. Dos Passos, on the contrary, can give all his attention to rendering a single life's special character. Each of his characters is unique; what happens to him could happen to no one else. What does it matter, since Society has marked him more deeply than could any special circumstance, since *he is* Society? Thus, we get a glimpse of an order beyond the accidents of fate or the contingency of detail, an order more supple than Zola's physiological necessity or Proust's psychological mechanism, a soft and insinuating constraint which seems to release its victims, letting them go only to take possession of them again without their suspecting, in other words, a statistical determinism. These men, submerged in their own existences, live as they can. They struggle; what comes their way is not determined in advance. And yet, neither their efforts, their faults, nor their most extreme violence can interfere with the regularity of births, marriages and suicides. The pressure exerted by a gas on the walls of its container does not depend upon the individual histories of the molecules composing it.

We are still on the other side of the looking-glass. Yesterday you saw your best friend and expressed to him your passionate hatred of war. Now try to relate this conversation to yourself in the style of Dos Passos. "And they ordered two beers and said that war was hateful. Paul declared he would rather do anything than fight and John said he agreed with him and both got excited and said they were glad they agreed. On his way home, Paul decided to see John more often." You will start hating yourself immediately. It will not take you long, however, to decide that you *cannot* use this tone in talking about yourself. However insincere you may have been, you were at least living out your insincerity, playing it out on your own, continuously creating and extending its existence from one moment to the next. And even if you got caught up in collective representations, you had first to experience them as personal resignation. We are neither mechanical objects nor possessed souls, but something worse; we are free. We exist either entirely *within* or entirely *without*. Dos Passos' man is a hybrid creature, an interior-exterior being. We go on living with him and within him, with his vacillating, individual consciousness, when suddenly it wavers, weakens, and is diluted in the collective consciousness. We follow it up to that point and suddenly, before we notice, we are on the outside. The man behind the looking-glass is a strange, contemptible, fascinating creature. Dos Passos knows how to use this constant shifting to fine effect. I know of nothing more gripping than Joe's death.

> Joe laid out a couple of frogs and was backing off towards the door, when he saw in the mirror that a big guy in a blouse was bringing down a bottle on his head held with both hands. He tried to swing around but he didn't have time. The bottle crashed his skull and he was out.

We are inside with him, until the shock of the bottle on his skull. Then immediately, we find ourselves outside with the chorus, part of the collective memory, ". . . and he was out." Nothing gives you a clearer feeling of annihilation. And from then on, each page we turn, each page that tells of other minds and of a world going on without Joe, is like a spadeful of earth over our bodies. But it is a behind-the-looking-glass death: all we really get is the fine *appearance* of nothingness. True nothingness can neither be felt nor thought. Neither you nor I, nor anyone after us, will ever have anything to say about our real deaths.

Dos Passos' world—like those of Faulkner, Kafka and Stendhal —is impossible because it is contradictory. But therein lies its beauty. Beauty is a veiled contradiction. I regard Dos Passos as the greatest writer of our time.

The Day of the Locust
by Nathanael West, 1939

The Stanley Rose Book Shop was a gathering place for fiction writers like Faulkner and West, who came to write for Hollywood during the Depression years. In his introduction to The Day of the Locust, *screenwriter and novelist Budd Schulberg, another Rose habitué, recalls twenty-four years later the man and the milieu that produced "this risible and terrifying little masterpiece."*

Nathanael West was one of the regulars who hung around the Stanley Rose Book Shop twenty-five years ago. Stanley Rose wasn't one of the characters in West's little time bomb of a Hollywood novel, *The Day of the Locust,* but he might have been. "Pep," as West was known to his friends, loved Stanley, and though Stanley had his favorites among the writers who made his bookstore on Hollywood Boulevard their home away from home (Bill Saroyan was one, this habitué another), we had to concede that Pep was Stanley's real favorite. Of the motley platoon of fiction writers who found temporary or permanent haven in Hollywood against the cold winds of Depression, Pep West was one of the handful Stanley liked to see after hours (such hours as Stanley kept) and on weekends. During hunting season their weekends might begin on Thursday and stretch into Tuesday. They were a pair of indefatigable hunters who seemed to work up much more passion in the pursuit of doves and ducks than in the discussion of Proust and Faulkner.

Faulkner would have been the first to agree with them; in fact, he even might have accompanied them. Another familiar face at Stanley's in his screen-writing days, Bill Faulkner shared with Rose and West the hunter's natural inclination to be unliterary—even antiliterary. Aside from Faulkner I can't recall any other men in the book business who leaned away from *talk* about books as determinedly as Pep West and Stanley Rose. Hemingway affected the antiliterary attitude but he had a penchant for talking about the writers he resented and thus could be led down the jungle path to literature. But West and Rose were consistent in their resistance to discussion of books. "Read anything good lately?" a writer just in from New York innocently asked Stanley Rose. "Me? I hate books!" "Then why do you run a bookstore?" "Because I like to keep a joint for pals to hang out in," Stanley explained.

Stanley liked to protest that he never read the books he sold and that he despised the literary types who ran up charge accounts at his hangout next door to Musso & Frank's, the friendly restaurant where needy writers could always eat for free simply by signing Stanley's name. Saroyan ate thousands of dollars' worth on Stanley's tab but, unlike some other recipients of this informal Stanley Rose Fellowship, Bill didn't forget his benefactor: he cut him in for ten per cent of the swag when he sold *The Human Comedy* to the movies. Stanley didn't like people to talk about his largesse for fear he would be accused of being a patron of the arts. He insisted he liked West mainly because Pep was always ready to go hunting, that he liked Saroyan because Bill was always ready to go gambling, and that he liked Faulkner for his readiness to drink sour mash whiskey and for his know-how with a shotgun. I was admitted to this inner circle not for the short stories I had begun to publish but because I knew my way around the Main Street gym and hung out with prizefighters.

It was Pep West who exposed Stanley Rose as a secret reader. "When hunting season is over Stanley likes to make us think that he devotes his weekends to whiskey and women. But he'll hole up, secretly, and read half a dozen books between Friday and Monday. I've even seen him carry a book along on our hunting trips." Stanley swore that Pep was defaming his character. And in a sense he was, for Stanley's public character drew its vitality, if not validity, from his reputation as a hard-drinking, hard-cussing, hard-wenching Texan who didn't give a damn for literature.

What was Nathanael West like in those years (1936–1940)

when we gathered in Stanley's backroom art gallery and drank Stanley's orange wine and talked politics, shoptalk and life? In preparation for this welcome to a timely new edition of *The Day of the Locust* I scribbled a free-association list of adjectives that describe Pep West: hulking, big, awkward, melancholy, sad, strange, detached, withdrawn, shy, friendly, warm, remote, secretive, shaggy, tweedy, gentle. To check my memory I phoned a survivor of the Stanley Rose days, who worked in his shop as a young girl and is now one of Hollywood's most prominent literary agents.

"What words come to mind when I think of Pep?" She paused. "Sad. Everything about him was sad. Even his mustache was sad. And melancholy. Strange. Detached." I didn't prompt her. "And at the same time," she went on, "he was terribly warm and friendly, but in a strange, detached way. Oh, and gentle. I remember him as terribly gentle."

What made Pep West such a curiosity in the gregarious backroom world of Stanley Rose's was the emotional and artistic poise he achieved through detachment. The climate of Hollywood in the late thirties, like the jazz of the period, was hot rather than cool, reflecting the restless political temper of the country. The Hollywood Anti-Nazi League could rally all but a Fascist minority for a spirited boycott of a dinner honoring Hitler's pet photographer, Leni Riefenstahl. Movie stars were raising funds for the striking lettuce workers of Salinas. When André Malraux came to town to raise funds for the Spanish Loyalists he out-glamor-boyed Robert Taylor, Gary Cooper and Cary Grant. Hollywood writers marched in the ranks of Harry Bridges' striking longshoremen and flocked to the Communist-oriented American Writers Congress. Some of the more prominent even joined the party itself, standing by their swimming pools with clenched fists, looking toward that "better world in birth" where beckoned that benign social engineer, "Uncle Joe" Stalin. There were strike novels by the yard that were analyzed and appreciated with intense—if not profound—seriousness at fellow-traveling cocktail parties and secret cell meetings. Socialist Realism, as exemplified by the most recent Soviet Writers Congress, was clearly the road to literary Nirvana.

How did the novelist Nathanael West adapt to this insistent drive toward political art? Refusing to involve himself in any of the fashionable polemics of his day, he simply went his own route. In a time when it was demanded of writers that they align themselves with "the progressive forces" in order to write "significantly," Pep West was an anomaly. While he gave lip service and physical presence to the popular causes, he somehow remained a determined negativist in a world of literary boosterism. (Yes, the world was dark, clouded with unemployment, Fascism and war, nearly all our writers were saying, but once the *people* organize and stand up together, there will be pie in the sky and paradise on earth.)

In those Depression years it was a rare act of faith to swim upstream. Eight or nine of every ten critics were oriented to the Popular Front. The same people who now welcome a James Purdy for his sense of detachment and alienation were belaboring West for these very values or perceptions thirty years ago. With rare exceptions they failed to recognize his earlier novel, *Miss Lonelyhearts,* published in 1933, as an elegant little classic. It is, like its author, sad, melancholy and strange. There is love of man in it but despair for mankind. In an age of Boris Karloff pseudoterror, it had real terror in it. In the decade of the clenched fist and the confident comrades it cried out, to the readers who weren't there, "God save us all—if there is a God!"

This may sound overwrought, but only West's characters and content were overwrought; the whole was contained by the sure hand of an artist gifted with the unfamiliar quality of detachment-involvement. *Miss Lonelyhearts* is the five-leaf clover, the perfect short novel, as flawless as F. Scott Fitzgerald's *The Great Gatsby,* as soul-disturbing as Thomas Mann's *Death in Venice.* Happily, this deeply unhappy book has survived the time-capsuled critics who neglected or ignored it (just as they badly missed the target on another novel by Fitzgerald, one of West's friends and admirers, whose *Tender Is the Night* was another "failure" of the hard-nosed thirties).

Nathanael West was as unique and uncelebrated to his time and place as was Franz Kafka to the late nineteenth century of

Middle Europe. Kafka was a neurasthenic little Jew from ghetto Europe; West (born Weinstein) was a big, tweedy, Ivy League Jew from a prosperous New York family. When Kafka thought of guns he thought of pogroms; to the Americanized Pep West of our leisure-loving, sports-indulging culture, guns were an avocation, a hobby and a companion on the prowl for small game in the rolling hills of Bucks County and the valleys of Lower California. Yet, strangely, this widely separated pair shared a dark vision of man in a frenzy of futility, like a beetle on its back. Man flails, man gropes, man scrambles for identity, man sweats to pull himself hand over hand toward the prize of dignity at the top of the pole. But in the dizzy climb man falters, loses his grip, slips and slides and tumbles in a grotesque acrobatic that becomes ever more ridiculous. You look at man and you can't help laughing until you cry. That's how I read Franz Kafka and Nathanael West.

On the strength of *Miss Lonelyhearts*, West was an inside celebrity to a group of us at Stanley Rose's. He was writing between assignments as a scenarist of run-of-the-mill Westerns at one of the B studios. Working on his own stuff, he was a meticulous craftsman, and he was rewriting and then rerewriting the small novel that was taking form slowly and surely. It was *The Day of the Locust*. The combined sale of his three previous books hardly would have kept him in cigarette money, but he had a devoted little band of followers at Stanley's waiting patiently for the new novel.

Elsewhere it has been written of West that he was beginning to rise on the Hollywood totem and that he might have developed into an "important" screenwriter. But Pep had few illusions about the Hollywood hand that fed him. Saroyan, who played irrepressible optimist to West's bone-deep pessimist, might look to the day when mighty MGM would allow him to cast his Fresno Armenian pipe dreams up there on the silver screen. But Pep had no ambition, no appetite for the movies, though his tender and savage nightmares might have made exciting offbeat film fare.

"I don't mind doing those oaters at Republic," he told me in the backroom gallery over a glass of wine one afternoon. "I watch my friends struggling to get their social messages into their million-dollar situation comedies and it seems to me it takes too much out of them—that is, if they hope to have anything left for their own work. The higher up you get on the screenwriting ladder the more they expect from you. This way I can write, 'Pardner, when you say that, smile,' and it's relatively painless and I can concentrate on what I want to write for myself."

Vividly I recall the afternoon the first copies of *The Day of the Locust* arrived at Stanley Rose's. It may seem irrelevant, but Pep, whose philosophic calm could be disturbed by unexpected things, was outraged at the color of the book jacket, a bright, garish red. "I'm going to kill that Bennett Cerf," he said, referring to our mutual publisher at Random House. "What a cheap, lousy-looking jacket!" Stanley Rose and I and a few others tried to reassure Pep that the jacket wasn't quite the tragic failure it seemed to him; that particular day he was not to be consoled. I asked him to autograph the book for me and he wrote, fretfully, "For Budd—When the day comes we can use it for a flag—Pep."

Stanley made a proud little pyramid of the red-jacketed copies in a place of honor in the window; his was undoubtedly the only bookstore in America to give this book its due. But neither a more distinguished jacket nor a favored place in all the bookstore windows of America would have helped *The Day of the Locust* in 1939. In a letter to Scott Fitzgerald, Pep summed up the critical reaction: "So far the box score stands: Good reviews—fifteen per cent, bad reviews—twenty-five per cent, brutal personal attacks—sixty per cent." Yet the book seemed to some of us at the time a worthy companion to *Miss Lonelyhearts,* an uncanny little novel, so irresistible in its wild daring and originality that not only do you not put it down; you are tempted to turn right back to page one and read it through again.

How sad for the critics and the readers that they were not there to greet it the first time around. For personal reasons I remember how poorly it sold. When I brought my first novel to Bennett Cerf shortly afterward he said, "Oh, no, not another Hollywood novel. You know what happened with Pep West's? It's a damned interesting little novel, but we'll be lucky if we sell fifteen hundred copies."

For contributing this risible and terrifying little masterpiece to our permanent library, Nathanael West earned the grand sum of $500—or roughly what he received for one week of writing "They-went-that-away" dialogue for the movies. Other writers I knew would have been upset by this neglect. But Pep bore his burden with uncommon objectivity. His emotions were geared to neglect.

When I returned to *The Day of the Locust* recently, to hone myself for this reappreciation, I did so with a sense of trepidation. I had reviewed the novel for *The New York Times* years ago, but how often have you read books once loved that crumbled in your hands on second or third reading? Was *The Day of the Locust* a mirage? What if it no longer enveloped me as it did when I first moved into it a quarter-century ago?

No sweat, as we say nowadays. From the opening pages I was drawn back into this bleak fantasy of life in the lower depths of the Hollywood inferno. There was the Westian boardinghouse, "the color of diluted mustard," with its "pink Moorish columns which supported turnip-shaped lintels." There was the outrageous, arrogant dwarf, Abe Kusich, the local bookie. And Faye Greener, who is all the teen-age voluptuaries who ever flung themselves at the studio gates; how deftly West rolled them all into one delicious, malicious bundle. And her father, the ex-vaudevillian to end them all, reduced to selling silver polish door to door, for whom every strange hallway is a stage as he hams his way into the grave. His death scene, with his daughter indulging in narcissistic primping with her back to him, is only one of a hilarious collection of mad vignettes.

For what makes this book so special is West's absolutely original way of illuminating his dark canvas with lightning flashes of wild humor. Here is the true gallows humor, which so often seems forced and self-consciously sensational in the currently fashionable theater and in the novel of the absurd that West foreshadowed. Just as in the thirties we had "premature anti-Fascists," punished for their sins of anti-Nazism before Western society as a whole was ready to commit itself, so Nathanael West clearly was guilty of premature absurdism, premature pessimism, premature alienationism. In the irresistible search for literary continuity, one might point to Nathanael West as the American from whom derive Carson McCullers, Joseph Heller, James Purdy and other poets of perversity in the soul-shocked nineteen sixties. West is a stylist able to shift ingeniously from far-out comedy to concentrated realism. This book brings you a cockfight, for instance, that Hemingway could not have described more cleanly blow by blow. And the final scene, the orgiastic riot of rootless thousands drawn to a hyped-up Hollywood premiere, is realism, God help us, carried that one step beyond the limits of reality that separates art from naturalism.

The orgiastic crowd, loving you this moment, destroying you the next, is the very essence of Hollywood—as Hollywood may be the essence of our success-driven culture. How truly West has caught it and recorded it in acid. What a brainstorm of an ending for the only Hollywood Gothic novel.

Soon after the publication of this book Pep West courted and wed a marvellous girl, Eileen McKenney. She had that unmistakable Irish-colleen beauty and she was hearty, funny, warm, outgoing, constitutionally cheerful and loving. She seemed to be the ideal extrovert to match his introversion, and his friends were gladdened to note the change in him. One night in the spring of 1940 I did the town with Pep and Eileen, hitting the jazz joints along Hollywood Boulevard and the Sunset Strip. Pep drank and sang and laughed and even accepted an impromptu jitterbug lesson from Eileen on the dance floor. We had never seen him so carefree and uninhibited. She seemed to be overhauling his entire personality. A rival (and possibly jealous) writer was only half joking when he speculated that the new Pep might get so happy that he would "lose that whole crazy, despairing thing" that set his work apart.

Alas. Alas. We will never know. Because Pep and Eileen were killed in an automobile accident after only a few months of marriage. Pep was a notorious, absent-minded and, if I remember correctly, nearsighted driver. The tragic accident, just one day after the untimely death of Scott Fitzgerald, Pep's friend and longtime encourager, left all their friends in a state of shock. It is my hunch that a more fulfilled, better adjusted Pep West would have gone on to ever greater works, just as I thought Fitzgerald's most mature work might have been ahead of him, if only he could have hung on. But Scott was at the far edge of his physical resources. Pep was in his prime. One eye was focused on the tragedy of cornered modern man, the other on the comedy, with the double image blended in a rare, apocalyptic vision. What a shelf of books he might have given us in his next thirty-six years!

But meanwhile, as we trudge or watusi on toward our destiny, we should be grateful for large pleasures in small packages—as The Book of Job is a small package and *Candide* is a small package, as are *A Season in Hell, Fontamara, Miss Lonelyhearts* and *The Day of the Locust*. We should be grateful for the small but incomparable body of work bequeathed us by the satanic, God-searching genius of Nathanael West.

DAVID BRADLEY ON

Native Son
by Richard Wright, 1940

In his introduction to a new edition of Richard Wright's Native Son, *a young black novelist talks about coming to terms with a brilliant predecessor whose landmark book he initially hated, and then—fifteen years and four readings later—grew to appreciate as the sad document of a different time. The essay that appears here was adapted from the original for the* New York Times Magazine *in 1986.*

I first began Richard Wright's *Native Son* in the winter of 1971, when, as an undergraduate at the University of Pennsylvania, I was taking a course called "Readings in Black Literature."

I had recently abandoned my major in English and invented one in "Creative Writing," which required me to produce a novel good enough to convince a faculty committee that I should get a degree. The problem was I couldn't be sure that anybody around—myself included—knew what a good novel, in my case, was. The cause of the uncertainty was the black esthetic.

The concept had been debated in black intellectual circles for almost a century, but in the late nineteen sixties and early seventies the idea that the art of black people ought to be created and judged by different standards from the art of white people had become an article of faith. One formulation of this notion had been articulated by James T. Stewart, a Philadelphia musician, in a 1966 essay, "The Development of the Black Revolutionary Artist."

"The dilemma of the 'negro' artist," Stewart had written, "is that he makes assumptions based on . . . white models. These assumptions are not only wrong, they are even antithetical to his existence." Stewart said that the black artist must "be estranged from the dominant culture. . . . This means that he cannot be 'successful' in any sense that has meaning in white critical evaluations. . . . In our movement toward the future, 'ineptitude' and 'unfitness' will be an aspect of what we do."

My dilemma was that at the University of Pennsylvania, white definitions of "ineptitude" and "unfitness" were rigorously applied. Still, I thought, I might already be a brilliant black writer, unrecognized because my work was being judged according to inappropriate standards. I took "Readings in Black Literature" hoping to discover that was so, or if it wasn't, hoping to make it so by learning from the classics of my people. One of these, of course, was *Native Son.*

Although I had never read *Native Son,* I had long been aware of it. In the politically charged atmosphere of a late-sixties campus, any black who wanted to be taken seriously had to be able to invoke the names of black writers, musicians and scholars whenever it was appropriate—and sometimes when it was not. And I had occasionally run across references to *Native Son.* I knew, for example, of Irving Howe's declaration that "the day *Native Son* appeared, American culture was changed forever," and I had seen the contents page of David Littlejohn's *Black on White: A Critical Survey of Writing by American Negroes,* which had sections headed "Before *Native Son:* The Dark Ages" and "Before *Native Son:* The Renaissance and After." Also, since I wanted to be a writer, I was acutely aware that *Native Son* was the first book published in America to make a black author a lot of money. I therefore opened it with great expectations. Like Dickens's Pip, I was terribly disappointed.

Put simply, I hated *Native Son.* Put more accurately, I hated it with a passion. Hated it because it violated most of the principles of novelistic construction I was struggling to master. The plot was improbable, the narrative voice intrusive, the language often stilted and the characters—especially that silly little rich white tease Mary Dalton and her stupid, gigolo Communist boyfriend, Jan—were stereotypical beyond belief. At first I tried to rationalize these flaws as precisely the "ineptitude" and "unfitness" that James T. Stewart had written about. But I couldn't get around what I hated with a passion: Bigger Thomas.

It wasn't that Bigger failed as a character, exactly. I had read Wright's essay "How Bigger Was Born," and therefore knew that Wright had set out to write a book "no one would weep over." In this, for me, Wright succeeded; I shed no tears for Bigger. I wanted him dead; by legal means if possible, by lynching if necessary. (The only difference between me and the mob that pursued him was that I hated him not because he had accidentally killed Mary— I *understood* that, and would have preferred it to have been intentional—but because he had intentionally murdered Bessie, a woman who loved him and would have done almost anything for him.) But I knew, too, that Wright had intended Bigger to be a flat character, so he could serve as a "meaningful and prophetic symbol" of the black masses. In this, for me, Wright failed. I did not see Bigger Thomas as a symbol of any kind of black man. To me he was a sociopath, pure and simple, beyond sympathy or understanding. The truth is, my first reading of *Native Son* ended at the passage in which Bigger, after practically raping Bessie, bashing in her face with a brick and tossing her body down an airshaft, thought that "he was living, truly and deeply." This, I thought, is sick.

I said so in class. I felt guilty about saying it, because all my life I had been schooled never to say a mumblin' word about any Negro the non-Negro world recognized as an achiever, which surely meant Richard Wright. I silently endured my classmates' charge that I had been so brainwashed by the dominant culture that I was "not black enough" to appreciate *Native Son*. I did not even protest (though I thought about it) that it was the dominant culture which had declared *Native Son* a work of brilliance. I kept my mouth shut because my heresy went beyond *Native Son*. I hated the idea of "Black Literature," too, and was resolved that if the price of becoming a black writer was following the model of *Native Son,* I would just have to write like a honky.

Fortunately, I found in works by other blacks—Charles Chesnutt, Jean Toomer, Zora Neale Hurston—reason to soften that stand. Still, reading *Native Son* made me determined that the models I took from black letters would come from the days before *Native Son* changed America and made Richard Wright a lot of money.

I first finished *Native Son* in the fall of 1973, when I was a graduate student at the University of London, ostensibly doing research for a thesis on the relationship between American history and the writing of American blacks.

I say "ostensibly" because I was actually hiding out in the British Museum and reading the essays of James Baldwin. Some of the essays, of course, were about *Native Son.*

Baldwin expressed eloquently the things I had tried to express in class. In "Everybody's Protest Novel" he charged that the works belonging to the sub-genre known as the protest novel, such as Harriet Beecher Stowe's *Uncle Tom's Cabin* and Wright's *Native Son,* were unreasonably forgiven "whatever violence they do to language, whatever excessive demands they make of credibility. It is, indeed, considered the sign of a frivolity so intense as to approach decadence to suggest that these books are badly written and wildly improbable." In *Many Thousands Gone,* Baldwin criticized *Native Son* in particular. "A necessary dimension," he wrote, "has been cut away; this dimension being the relationship that Negroes bear to one another. . . . It is this which has led us all to believe that in Negro life there exists no tradition, no field of manners, no possibility of ritual or intercourse. . . ." Aha! I thought triumphantly. Who is going to tell James Baldwin he isn't black enough?

But Baldwin did something more significant than rescue my claim to racial identity: in arguing that the flaws in *Native Son* were common to novels distinguished not by the race of the author but by the form of the work, Baldwin, in effect, was challenging the black esthetic. This made me realize that although a course in black literature had made it possible for me to read works by black authors which were otherwise absent from the curriculum, the assumptions behind the course had made it impossible for me to see those works as part of an American, as opposed to Afro-American, literary tradition. I wondered if I would have a different reaction to *Native*

Son if I considered it in a new context. So I went in search of a copy.

My reaction was indeed different. Put simply, *Native Son* infuriated me. Put sequentially, it bemused, astonished, horrified and then infuriated me. And then it frightened me out of my wits.

The British Museum had a copy of the original edition of *Native Son* which included an introduction by Dorothy Canfield. It seemed curious that a contemporary novel would require an introduction at all. But especially *that* introduction. For, while Canfield said things you would expect an introducer to say, testifying that "the author shows genuine literary skill in the construction of his novel," and comparing him to Dostoyevsky, she also said things you would expect an introducer *not* to say—for example, that she "did not at all mean to imply that *Native Son* as literature is comparable to the masterpieces of Dostoyevsky . . ." What was horrifying was what she thought Wright's novel *was* comparable to.

"How to produce neuroses in sheep and psychopathic upsets in rats and other animals has been known to research scientists for so long that accounts of these experiments have filtered out to us, the general public," she began, and went on that "our society puts Negro youth in the situation of the animal in the psychological laboratory in which a neurosis is to be caused." *Native Son,* she said, was "the first report in fiction we have had from those who succumb to these distracting crosscurrents of contradictory nerve impulses, from those whose behavior patterns give evidence of the same bewildered, senseless tangle of abnormal nerve-reactions studied in animals by psychologists in laboratory experiments."

Suddenly I realized that many readers of *Native Son had* seen Bigger Thomas as a symbol; in 1940, when *Native Son* hit the shelves, they, like Mary Dalton, had probably never come into enough contact with blacks to know better. God, I thought, they think we're all Biggers.

I found myself wondering how many of the attitudes of nineteen forties whites toward blacks may have been confirmed, influenced, if not totally shaped by such a tremendously popular "report." Had

Native Son contributed to the facts that, in 1942, less than half of all white Americans approved of integrated transportations facilities, and that only about one in three approved of integrated schools or neighborhoods? And, if they believed *Native Son* was an accurate "report," who could blame them for those attitudes? I myself did not want a nut like Bigger Thomas sitting next to me on a bus or in a schoolroom, and certainly I did not want him moving in next door.

Still, I thought, while Canfield's characterization may have seemed credible to the general public, it seemed incredible to me that literary critics would have accepted it. So I sought out Irving Howe's essay, "Black Boys and Native Sons," from which the "changed the world" quote had come. In Howe, I thought, I'd surely find someone who knew that a novel is not a report.

But Howe was just as bad. True, he praised *Native Son* for having changed our culture, but he also wrote of "all its crudeness, melodrama and claustrophobia of vision. . . . The language is often coarse, flat in rhythm, syntactically overburdened, heavy with journalistic slag . . . *Native Son*, though preserving some of the devices of the naturalistic novel, deviates sharply from its characteristic tone: a tone Wright could not possibly have maintained and which, it may be, no Negro novelist can really hold for long."

At that moment I saw how *Native Son* could be a classic according to the black esthetic and still be loved by white critics; the whites did not view it as literature, except in the sense that scientific journals or polemical pamphlets are literature.

I saw, too, how unmarked was the road I would have to travel if I became a writer. I could not assume I was writing well if white critics praised my work or if they slammed it for "ineptitude" and "unfitness." They might praise it to the skies while finding it inept and unfit, for they might think me not a writer but a laboratory rat just slightly more articulate than his fellows.

I opened *Native Son* for the third time in the summer of 1977. By then I had written a novel called *South Street*. Acclaimed as a "black novel," it prompted a magazine editor to invite me to review a "new" book by Richard Wright—who had died in Paris in 1960 and had been cremated with a copy of his autobiography, *Black Boy*, at his side. The appearance of the "new" book was due not to reincarnation, but to the curious publication history of *Black Boy*.

Black Boy, published in March 1945, told the story of Wright's youth in the oppressive South and his escape to the North. As he wrote in the book's concluding lines, he made his escape with his head "full of a hazy notion that life could be lived with dignity, that the personalities of others should not be violated, that men should be able to confront other men without fear or shame. . . ." The book was a huge success—400,000 copies were sold within weeks. This was perhaps due to the fact that Wright's escape, which conformed to the pattern of the "Great Migration" of blacks during the first third of the century, when coupled with his wealth and fame, made *Black Boy* the quintessential Afro-American success story.

But it hadn't been that when Wright completed it in 1943, calling it *American Hunger*. In this version, Wright had gone on to describe the experiences in the North that shaped the pessimism of *Native Son*—his near-starvation in the Chicago ghetto, his lonely drive toward self-education, his Kafkaesque involvement with the Communist Party. Sometime in mid-1944, however, Wright's editor at Harper & Brothers, Edward C. Aswell, told Wright he felt "the book would break much more logically with the departure from the South." Wright originally told his agent, Paul Reynolds, Jr., "I don't think that there is much I will ever be able to do on this script. . . . The thing will have to stand as it is." Still he agreed not only to cut almost a third of the manuscript, but also to alter the tone by adding five concluding pages that contained that hopeful "hazy notion." The deleted portion remained essentially unpublished until 1977; this was the book I was asked to review.

My response to the story behind *American Hunger* mirrored my reactions to the British Museum's copy of *Native Son*: bemusement, that Wright—or anybody—should write an autobiography at thirty-two; astonishment, at his editor's effrontery in asking that the text of that autobiography be truncated; horror, at Wright's acquiescence and cooperation. The fury came as I read *American Hunger*, which seemed to me a virtual rewriting of *Native Son*. What inspired that fury was not the many similarities between Wright's history and Bigger's, but the presence of a real-life Bessie.

At one point Wright earned a living selling burial insurance in the Chicago ghetto, where, as he wrote in *American Hunger,* "there were many comely black housewives who . . . were willing to make bargains to escape paying a ten-cent premium each week." Wright made such a "bargain." While he did not bash in the woman's face with a brick, he did once threaten to kill her, laughed at her when she admired his ability with words and viewed her as a sex object. "Sex relations were the only relations she had ever had," he wrote. "No others were possible with her, so limited was her intelligence." Once, "I stared at her and wondered just what a life like hers meant in the scheme of things, and I came to the conclusion that it meant absolutely nothing."

Black folks have a word for a man who could even think something like that about a woman whose bed he's shared: cold. And that was the image of Wright that came to me as I read *American Hunger* and went back to read *Black Boy*. In both books I could see Wright, the frigid intellectual, portraying black people as psychological "types"—and then damning them for their lack of humanity. In *Black Boy,* he wrote of his father, "how fastened were his memories to a crude and raw past, how chained were his actions and emotions to the direct, animalistic impulses of his withering body." Of black people in general, he wrote, "I used to mull over the strange absence of real kindness in Negroes, how unstable was our tenderness, how lacking in genuine passion we were, how void of great hope, how timid our joy, how bare our traditions, how hollow our memories, how lacking we were in those intangible sentiments that bind man to man, and how shallow was even our despair. . . . I saw that what had been taken for our emotional strength was our negative confusions, our flights, our fears, our frenzy under pressure."

In those passages I heard echoes of *Native Son*. What made me furious was not that the novel was autobiographical—an artist has a right to draw his material from wherever he chooses—but that

Wright had to know these statements were untrue. But he also knew how much they conformed to the view of blacks that prevailed in the very society he accused of oppression, for, in *American Hunger* he wrote that "My reading in sociology had enabled me to discern many strange types of Negro characters." Put kindly, it seemed to me that Wright was pandering to white expectations. Put bluntly, I thought he had sold his people down the river to make a buck.

But as I searched through *American Hunger* for the quotes to support that view, I saw something which, in my outrage, I had overlooked: that, after saying the life of his lover "meant absolutely nothing" Wright had gone on. "And neither did my life mean anything." The awful thought occurred to me. What if Richard Wright was not pandering to white expectations? What if he believed he was writing the truth? What then would be the meaning of *Native Son*?

My second full reading of *Native Son* filled me with a terrible sorrow. Not for Bigger Thomas—I still did not give a damn about him—but for Richard Wright himself. For when I read the passage in which Mary Dalton tells Bigger how she had long wanted to enter a ghetto house "and just see how your people live," I heard the echo of Dorothy Canfield's introduction. And in the passage in which Jan tells Bigger that it was really O.K. that Bigger had killed the woman he, Jan, loved, because "You believed enough to kill. You thought you were settling something or you wouldn't've killed," I heard Irving Howe's blithe waiver of the esthetic standards that he, as a critic, *had* to hold dear. And when Bigger, at the end of his life, reiterates that piece of dialectic insanity, I saw Richard Wright letting somebody tell him where his life logically ended.

And I realized that previously I had done *Native Son* the injustice of trying to fit it into my America, a place where, while a black person's right to human dignity is not exactly a given, such a thesis can at least be argued. Richard Wright's America was a different place, a place where a black who hoped to survive needed a sense of humility more than a sense of dignity, and where Bigger Thomas's story was no more melodramatic, crude or claustrophobic than the times themselves.

In Richard Wright's America, a novelist could—as Wright did—base descriptions of lynch mobs in the streets of Chicago on reports taken directly from newspapers. In Richard Wright's America, a best-selling financially independent novelist—if he was a Negro—could not lunch with his agent in a midtown Manhattan restaurant, could not buy a house in Greenwich Village and could only rent an apartment there if he found a landlord willing to defy half the neighborhood. In Richard Wright's America, a critically acclaimed, Guggenheim Fellowship–winning Negro novelist would hesitate to use the surnames of his agent and his editor in the dedication of a book because he was not sure they would want to be so closely associated with a black. In Richard Wright's America, they didn't have black literature courses; a black boy who wanted to be a writer could remain tragically unaware of the writing of black people, and could say, while explaining the origins of his characters, that "association with white writers was the life preserver of my hope to depict Negro life in fiction, for my race possessed no fictional works . . . no novels that went with a deep and fearless will down to the dark roots of life."

And so I came to realize that *Native Son* was not as inaccurate as I had thought; and that, in a sense, Dorothy Canfield was not entirely wrong. Not that there was great validity in Wright's use of Bigger Thomas as a type. Nor is there any validity in reading any piece of fiction as "a report" of general social conditions. But fiction *is* a report of specific conditions: that is its value. *Native Son,* I realized, shows the vision one black man held of his people, his country, and, ultimately, himself. And I thought, Dear God, how horrible for a man to have to write this. And, Please, God, let no one ever have to write this again.

It is the autumn of 1986. I have just finished reading *Native Son* for the fourth time. I have been invited to write an introduction to a new edition. Put simply—and frighteningly, to me—I have been asked to step into the role of Dorothy Canfield, and dared to do a better job.

I am not sure I can do a better job. For while what Canfield wrote still infuriates me, she was a part of her time, as I am a part of mine. Still, I have had the opportunity—as she did not—to read *Native Son* over a span of years. And I find that I can be kinder toward *Native Son* than I have been in the past.

Not that I think *Native Son* has suddenly become artistically brilliant. But I have realized, belatedly, that *Native Son* is a first novel. Its flaws are typical of first novels, no more severe than those found in most. And now I can see beneath the shroud of politics, and accept that *Native Son* is, in fact, a valuable document—not of sociology, but of history. It reminds us of a time in this land of freedom when a man could have this bleak and frightening vision of his people, and when we had so little contact with one another that the vision could be accepted as fact.

But despite that, I find that Wright, after all these years, has failed in an ironic way. He wanted *Native Son* to be a book "no one would weep over." With me, he once succeeded. He no longer does. *Native Son* is an ineffably sad expression of what once were the realities of this nation. We have not come as far as we ought. But I hope we have come far enough by now to read *Native Son* and weep.

TENNESSEE WILLIAMS ON

Reflections in a Golden Eye
by Carson McCullers, 1941

In 1946, Tennessee Williams wrote a letter to fellow southerner Carson McCullers praising her new novel, The Member of the Wedding, *and a friendship of "kindred souls" quickly developed between them. In this introduction to a 1949 edition, Williams takes her part against the early reviewers of* Reflections in a Golden Eye.

This book, *Reflections in a Golden Eye*, is a second novel, and although its appreciation has steadily risen during the eight or nine years since its first appearance, it was then regarded as somewhat disappointing in the way that second novels usually are. When the book preceding a second novel has been very highly acclaimed, as was *The Heart Is a Lonely Hunter*, there is an inclination on the part of critics to retrench their favor, so nearly automatic and invariable a tendency that it can almost be set down as a physical law. But the reasons for failure to justly evaluate this second novel go beyond the common, temporal disadvantage that all second novels must suffer, and I feel that an examination of these reasons may be of considerably greater pertinence to our aim of suggesting a fresh evaluation.

To quote directly from book-notices that came out over a decade ago is virtually impossible, here in Rome where I am writing these comments, but I believe that I am safe in assuming that it was their identification of the author with a certain school of American writers, mostly of southern origin, that made her subject to a particular and powerful line of attack.

Even in the preceding book some readers must undoubtedly have detected a warning predisposition toward certain elements which are popularly known as "morbid." Doubtless there were some critics, as well as readers, who did not understand why Carson McCullers had elected to deal with a matter so unwholesome as the spiritual but passionate attachment that existed between a deaf-mute and a half-wit. But the tenderness of the book disarmed them. The depth and nobility of its compassion were so palpable that at least for the time being the charge of decadence had to be held in check. This forbearance was of short duration. In her second novel the veil of a subjective tenderness, which is the one quality of her talent which she has occasionally used to some excess, was drawn away. And the young writer suddenly flashed in their faces the cabalistic emblems of fellowship with a certain company of writers that the righteous "Humanists" in the world of letters regarded as most abhorrent and most necessary to expose and attack.

Not being a follower of literary journals, I am not at all sure what title has been conferred upon this group of writers by their disparaging critics, but for my own convenience I will refer to them as the Gothic school. It has a very ancient lineage, this school, but our local inheritance of its tradition was first brought into prominence by the early novels of William Faulkner, who still remains a most notorious and unregenerate member. There is something in the region, something in the blood and culture, of the southern state that has somehow made them the center of this Gothic school of writers. Certainly something more important than the influence of a single artist, Faulkner, is to be credited with its development, just as in France the Existentialist movement is surely attributable to forces more significant than the personal influence of Jean-Paul Sartre. There is actually a common link between the two schools, French and American, but characteristically the motor impulse of the French school is intellectual and philosophic while that of the American is more of an emotional and romantic nature. What is this common link? In my opinion it is most simply definable as a sense, an intuition, of an underlying dreadfulness in modern experience.

The question one hears most frequently about writers of the Gothic school is this little classic:

"Why do they write about such *dreadful things?*"

This is a question that escapes not only from the astonished lips of summer matrons who have stumbled into the odd world of William Faulkner, through some inadvertence or mischief at the lending-library, but almost as frequently and certainly more importantly, from the pens of some of the most eminent book-critics. If it were a solely and typically philistine manifestation, there would be no sense or hope in trying to answer it, but the fact that it is used as a major line of attack by elements that the artist has to deal with—critics, publishers, distributors, not to mention the reading public—makes it a question that we should try seriously to answer or at least understand.

The great difficulty of understanding, and communication, lies in the fact that we who are asked this question and those who ask it do not really inhabit the same universe.

You do not need to tell me that this remark smacks of artistic snobbism which is about as unattractive as any other form that snobbism can take. (If artists are snobs, it is much in the same humble way that lunatics are: not because they wish to be different, and hope and believe that they are, but because they are forever painfully struck in the face with the inescapable fact of their difference which makes them hurt and lonely enough to want to undertake the vocation of artists.)

It appears to me, sometimes, that there are only two kinds of people who live outside what E. E. Cummings has defined as "this so-called world of ours"—the artists and the insane. Of course there are those who are not practicing artists and those who have not been committed to asylums, but who have enough of one or both magical elements, lunacy and vision, to permit them also to slip sufficiently apart from "this so-called world of ours" to undertake or accept an exterior view of it. But I feel that Mr. Cummings established a highly defensible point when he stated, at least by implication, that "the everyday humdrum world, which includes me and you and millions upon millions of men and women" is pretty largely something done with mirrors, and the mirrors are the millions of eyes that look at each other and things no more penetratingly than the physical senses allow. If they are conscious of there being anything to explore beyond this *soi-disant* universe, they comfortably suppose it to be represented by the mellow tones of the pipe-organ on Sundays.

In expositions of this sort it is sometimes very convenient to invent an opposite party to an argument, as Mr. Cummings did in making the remarks I have quoted. Such an invented adversary might say to me at this point:

"I have read some of these books, like this one here, and I think they're sickening and crazy. I don't know why anybody should want to write about such diseased and perverted and fantastic creatures and try to pass them off as representative members of the human race! That's how I feel about it. But I do have this sense you talk about, as much as you do or anybody else, this sense of fearfulness or dreadfulness or whatever you want to call it. I read the newspapers and I think it's all pretty awful. I think the atom bomb is awful and I think that the confusion of the world is awful. I think that cancer is fearful, and I certainly don't look forward to the idea of dying, which I think is dreadful. I could go on forever, or at least indefinitely, giving you a list of things that I think are dreadful. And isn't that having what you call the Sense of Dreadfulness or something?"

My hesitant answer would be—"Yes, and no. Mostly no."

And then I would explain a little further, with my usual awkwardness at exposition:

"All of these things that you list as dreadful are parts of the visible, sensible phenomena of every man's experience or knowledge, but the true sense of dread is not a reaction to anything sensible or visible or even, strictly, materially, *knowable*. But rather it's a kind of spiritual intuition of something almost too incredible and shocking to talk about, which underlies the whole so-called thing. It is the incommunicable something that we shall have to call *mystery* which is so inspiring of dread among these modern artists that we have been talking about. . . ."

Then I pause, looking into the eyes of my interlocutor which I hope are beginning to betray some desire to believe me, and I say to him, "Am I making any better sense?"

"Maybe. But I can see it's an effort!"

"My friend, you have me where the hair is short."

"But you know, you still haven't explained why these writers have to write about crazy people doing terrible things!"

"You mean the externals they use?"

" 'Externals?' "

"You are objecting to their choice of symbols."

"Symbols, are they?"

"Of course. Art is made out of symbols the way your body is made out of vital tissue."

"Then why have they got to use—?"

"Symbols of the grotesque and the violent? Because a book is short and a man's life is long."

"That I don't understand."

"Think it over."

"You mean it's got to be more concentrated?"

"Exactly. The awfulness has to be compressed."

"But can't a writer ever get the same effect without using such God damn awful subjects?"

"I believe one writer did. The greatest of modern times, James Joyce. He managed to get the whole sense of awfulness without resorting to externals that departed on the surface from the ordinary and the familiar. But he wrote very long books, when he accomplished this incredibly difficult thing, and also he used a device that is known as the interior monologue which only he and one other great modern writer could employ without being excessively tiresome."

"What other?"

"Marcel Proust. But Proust did not ever quite dare to deliver the message of Absolute Dread. He was too much of a physical coward. The atmosphere of his work is rather womb-like. The flight into protection is very apparent."

"I guess we've talked long enough. Don't you have to get back to your subject now?"

"I have just about finished with my subject, thanks to you."

"Aren't you going to make a sort of statement that adds it up?"

"Neatly? Yes. Maybe I'd better try: here it is: *Reflections in a Golden Eye* is one of the purest and most powerful of those works which are conceived in that Sense of The Awful which is the desperate black root of nearly all significant modern art, from the *Guernica* of Picasso to the cartoons of Charles Addams. Is that all right?"

"I have quit arguing with you. So long."

It is true that this book lacks somewhat the thematic magnitude of the *Chasseur Solitaire*, but there is an equally important respect in which it is superior.

The first novel had a tendency to overflow in places as if the virtuosity of the young writer had not yet fallen under her entire control. But in the second there is an absolute mastery of design. There is a lapidary precision about the structure of this second book. Furthermore I think it succeeds more perfectly in establishing its own reality, in creating a world of its own, and this is something that primarily distinguishes the work of a great artist from that of a professional writer. In this book there is perhaps no single passage that assaults the heart so mercilessly as that scene in the earlier novel where the deaf-mute Singer stands at night outside the squalid flat that he had formerly occupied with the crazed and now dying Antonopolous. The acute tragic sensibility of scenes like that occurred more frequently in *The Heart Is a Lonely Hunter*. Here the artistic climate is more austere. The tragedy is more distilled: a Grecian purity cools it, the eventually overwhelming impact is of a more reflective order. The key to this deliberate difference is implicit in the very title of the book. Discerning critics should have found it the opposite of a disappointment since it exhibited the one attribute which had yet to be shown in Carson McCullers' stunning array of gifts: the gift of mastery over a youthful lyricism.

I will add, however, that this second novel is still not her greatest; it is surpassed by *The Member of the Wedding*, her third novel, which combined the heart-breaking tenderness of the first with the sculptural quality of the second. But this book is in turn surpassed by a somewhat shorter work. I am speaking of *The Ballad of the Sad Cafe,* which is assuredly among the masterpieces of our language in the form of the novella. It has appeared, so far, only in the pages of a magazine of fashion and in an otherwise rather undistinguished anthology, which is now out of print. It is at present obtainable only after diligent search among the stalls of dealers in old magazines and remainders. But as I write these comments I am assured that it is soon to be re-issued in a volume of short stories.

During the two years that I have spent mostly abroad I have been impressed by the disparity that exists between Carson McCullers' reputation at home and in Europe. Translation serves as a winnowing process. The lesser and more derivative talents that have boisterously flooded our literary scene, with reputations inflated by professional politics and by shrewd commercial promotion, have somewhat obscured at home the position of more authentic talents. But in Europe the name of Carson McCullers is where it belongs, among the four or five preeminent figures in contemporary American writing.

Carson McCullers does not work rapidly. She is not coerced by the ridiculous popular idea that a good novelist turns out a book once a year. As long as five years elapsed between her second full-length novel and her third. I understand now that she has begun to work upon another. There could be no better literary news for any of us who have found, as I have found in her work, such intensity and nobility of spirit as we have not had in our prose-writing since Herman Melville. In the meantime she should be reassured by the constantly more abundant evidence that the work she has already accomplished, such as this work, is not eclipsed by time but further illumined.

Invisible Man
by Ralph Ellison, 1952

Invisible Man *earned Ralph Ellison the 1953 National Book Award as "the most distinguished work of fiction published in 1952." During the thirty-year life of that award, he was the only black American to be so honored. Saul Bellow, in his review for* Commentary, *called it "a book of the very first order" and wrote, "so many hands have been busy at the interment of the novel . . . that I can't help feeling elated when a resurrection occurs."*

A few years ago, in an otherwise dreary and better forgotten number of *Horizon* devoted to a louse-up of life in the United States, I read with great excitement an episode from *Invisible Man*. It described a free-for-all of blindfolded Negro boys at a stag party of the leading citizens of a small Southern town. Before being blindfolded the boys are made to stare at a naked white woman; then they are herded into the ring, and, after the battle royal, one of the fighters, his mouth full of blood, is called upon to give his high school valedictorian's address. As he stands under the lights of the noisy room, the citizens rib him and make him repeat himself; an accidental reference to equality nearly ruins him, but everything ends well and he receives a handsome briefcase containing a scholarship to a Negro college.

This episode, I thought, might well be the high point of an excellent novel. It has turned out to be not *the* high point but rather one of the many peaks of a book of the very first order, a superb book. The valedictorian is himself Invisible Man. He adores the college but is thrown out before long by its president, Dr. Bledsoe, a great educator and leader of his race, for permitting a white visitor to visit the wrong places in the vicinity. Bearing what he believes to be a letter of recommendation from Dr. Bledsoe he comes to New

York. The letter actually warns prospective employers against him. He is recruited by white radicals and becomes a Negro leader, and in the radical movement he learns eventually that throughout his entire life his relations with other men have been schematic; neither with Negroes nor with whites has he ever been visible, real. I think that in reading the *Horizon* excerpt I may have underestimated Mr. Ellison's ambition and power for the following very good reason, that one is accustomed to expect excellent novels about boys, but a modern novel about men is exceedingly rare. For this enormously complex and difficult American experience of ours very few people are willing to make themselves morally and intellectually responsible. Consequently, maturity is hard to find.

It is commonly felt that there is no strength to match the strength of those powers which attack and cripple modern mankind. And this feeling is, for the reader of modern fiction, all too often confirmed when he approaches a new book. He is prepared, skeptically, to find what he has found before, namely, that family and class, university, fashion, the giants of publicity and manufacture, have had a larger share in the creation of someone called a writer than truth or imagination—that Bendix and Studebaker and the nylon division of Du Pont, and the University of Chicago, or Columbia or Harvard or Kenyon College, have once more proved mightier than the single soul of an individual; to find that one more lightly manned position has been taken. But what a great thing it is when a brilliant individual victory occurs, like Mr. Ellison's, proving that a truly heroic quality can exist among our contemporaries. People too thoroughly determined—and our institutions by their size and force too thoroughly determine—can't approach this quality. That can only be done by those who resist the heavy influences and make their own synthesis out of the vast mass of phenomena, the seething, swarming body of appearances, facts, and details. From this harassment and threatened dissolution by details, a writer tries to rescue what is important. Even when he is most bitter, he makes by his tone a declaration of values and he says, in effect: "There is something nevertheless that a man may hope to be." This tone, in the best pages of *Invisible Man*, those pages, for instance, in which an incestuous Negro farmer tells his tale to a white New England philanthropist, comes through very powerfully; it is tragicomic, poetic, the tone of the very strongest sort of creative intelligence.

In a time of specialized intelligences, modern imaginative writers make the effort to maintain themselves as *un*specialists, and their quest is for a true middle-of-consciousness for everyone. What language is it that we can all speak, and what is it that we can all recognize, burn at, weep over; what is the stature we can without exaggeration claim for ourselves; what is the main address of consciousness?

I was keenly aware, as I read this book, of a very significant kind of independence in the writing. For there is a "way" for Negro novelists to go at their problems, just as there are Jewish or Italian "ways." Mr. Ellison has not adopted a minority tone. If he had done so, he would have failed to establish a true middle-of-consciousness for everyone.

Negro Harlem is at once primitive and sophisticated; it exhibits the extremes of instinct and civilization as few other American communities do. If a writer dwells on the peculiarity of this, he ends with an exotic effect. And Mr. Ellison is not exotic. For him this balance of instinct and culture or civilization is not a Harlem matter; it is *the* matter, German, French, Russian, American, universal, a matter very little understood. It is thought that Negroes and other minority people, kept under in the great status battle, are in the instinct cellar of dark enjoyment. This imagined enjoyment provokes envious rage and murder; and then it is a large portion of human nature itself which becomes the fugitive murderously pursued. In our society Man—Himself—is idolized and publicly worshipped, but the single individual must hide himself underground and try to save his desires, his thoughts, his soul, in invisibility. He must return to himself, learning self-acceptance and rejecting all that threatens to deprive him of his manhood.

This is what I make of *Invisible Man*. It is not by any means faultless; I don't think the hero's experiences in the Communist party are as original in conception as other parts of the book, and his love affair with a white woman is all too brief, but it is an immensely moving novel and it has greatness.

So many hands have been busy at the interment of the novel— the hand of Paul Valéry, the hands of the editors of literary magazines, of scholars who decide when genres come and go, the hands of innumerable pipsqueaks as well—that I can't help feeling elated when a resurrection occurs. People read history and then seem to feel that everything has to conclude in their own time. "We have read history, and therefore history is over," they appear to say. Really, all that such critics have the right to say is that fine novels are few and far between. That's perfectly true. But then fine anythings are few and far between. If these critics wanted to be extremely truthful, they'd say they were bored. Boredom, of course, like any mighty force, you must respect. There is something terribly impressive about the boredom of a man like Valéry who could no longer bear to read that the carriage had come for the duchess at four in the afternoon. And certainly there are some notably boring things to which we owe admiration of a sort.

Not all the gravediggers of the novel have such distinction as Valéry's, however. Hardly. And it's difficult to think of them as rising dazzled from a volume of Stendhal, exclaiming "God!" and then with angry determination seizing their shovels to go and heap more clods on the coffin. No, theirs unfortunately isn't often the disappointment of spirits formed under the influence of the masters. They make you wonder how, indeed, they *would* be satisfied. A recent contributor to *Partisan Review,* for instance, complains that modern fiction does not keep pace with his swift-wheeling modern consciousness which apparently leaves the photon far behind in its speed. He names a few *really* modern writers of fiction, their work unfortunately still unpublished, and makes a patronizing reference to *Invisible Man:* almost, but not quite, the real thing, it is "raw" and "overambitious." And the editors of *Partisan Review* who have published so much of this modern fiction that their contributor attacks, what do they think of this? They do not say what they think; neither of this piece nor of another lulu on the same subject and in the same issue by John Aldridge. Mr. Aldridge writes: "There are only two cultural pockets left in America, and they are the Deep South and that area of northeastern United States whose moral capital is Boston, Massachusetts. This is to say that these are the only places where there are any manners. In all other parts of the country people live in a kind of vastly standardized cultural prairie, a sort of infinite Middle West, and that means that they don't really live and they don't really do anything."

Most Americans thus are Invisible. Can we wonder at the cruelty of dictators when even a literary critic, without turning a hair, announces the death of a hundred million people?

Let us suppose that the novel is, as they say, played out. Let us only suppose it, for I don't believe it. But what if it is so? Will such tasks as Mr. Ellison has set himself no more be performed? Nonsense. New means, when new means are necessary, will be found. To find them is easier than to suit the disappointed consciousness and to penetrate the thick walls of boredom within which life lies dying.

ROBERT BRUSTEIN ON

Catch-22
by Joseph Heller, 1961

In an article celebrating the twenty-fifth anniversary of Catch-22, *John Aldridge characterized the various early critical responses to the novel as idiotic, puzzled, ambivalent, outraged, and prophetically perceptive. Of those in the last category, he offered special praise to this review by Robert Brustein originally entitled "The Logic of Survival in a Lunatic World," which appeared in* The New Republic *in 1961. He wrote that Brustein was "so superbly intelligent about the book that much of the later criticism has done little to improve his essential argument."*

Like all superlative works of comedy—and I am ready to argue that this is one of the most bitterly funny works in the language—*Catch-22* is based on an unconventional but utterly convincing internal logic. In the very opening pages, when we come upon a number of Air Force officers malingering in a hospital—one censoring all the modifiers out of enlisted men's letters and signing the censor's name "Washington Irving," another pursuing tedious conversations with boring Texans in order to increase his life span by making time pass slowly, still another storing horse chestnuts in his cheeks to give himself a look of innocence—it seems obvious that an inordinate number of Joseph Heller's characters are, by all conventional standards, mad. It is a triumph of Mr. Heller's skill that he is so quickly able to persuade us (1) that the most lunatic are the most logical, and (2) that it is our conventional standards which lack any logical consistency. The sanest looney of them all is the apparently harebrained central character, an American bombardier of Syrian extraction named Captain John Yossarian, who is based on a mythical Italian island (Pianosa) during World War II. For while many of his fellow officers seem indifferent to their own survival, and most of his superior

officers are overtly hostile to his, Yossarian is animated solely by a
desperate determination to stay alive:

> It was a vile and muddy war, and Yossarian could have lived without
> it—lived forever, perhaps. Only a fraction of his countrymen would give
> up their lives to win it, and it was not his ambition to be among them. . . .
> That men would die was a matter of necessity; *which* men would die,
> though, was a matter of circumstance, and Yossarian was willing to be
> the victim of anything but circumstance.

The single narrative thread in this crazy patchwork of anec-
dotes, episodes, and character portraits traces Yossarian's herculean
efforts—through caution, cowardice, defiance, subterfuge, strate-
gem, and subversion, through feigning illness, goofing off, and poi-
soning the company's food with laundry soap—to avoid being
victimized by circumstance, a force represented in the book as
Catch-22. For Catch-22 is the unwritten loophole in every written
law which empowers the authorities to revoke your rights whenever
it suits their cruel whims; it is, in short, the principle of absolute
evil in a malevolent, mechanical, and incompetent world. Because
of Catch-22, justice is mocked, the innocent are victimized, and
Yossarian's squadron is forced to fly more than double the number
of missions prescribed by Air Force code. Dogged by Catch-22,
Yossarian becomes the anguished witness to the ghoulish slaughter
of his crew members and the destruction of all his closest friends,
until finally his fear of death becomes so intense that he refuses to
wear a uniform, after his own has been besplattered with the guts
of his dying gunner, and receives a medal standing naked in for-
mation. From this point on Yossarian's logic becomes so pure that
everyone thinks him mad, for it is the logic of sheer survival, dedicated to keeping him alive in a world noisily clamoring for his
annihilation.

According to this logic, Yossarian is surrounded on all sides by
hostile forces: his enemies are distinguished less by their nationality
than by their ability to get him killed. Thus, Yossarian feels a blind,
electric rage against the Germans whenever they hurl flak at his
easily penetrated plane; but he feels an equally profound hatred for

those of his own countrymen who exercise an arbitrary power over his life and well-being. Heller's huge cast of characters, therefore, is dominated by a large number of comic malignities, *genus Americanus*, drawn with a grotesqueness so audacious that they somehow transcend caricature entirely and become vividly authentic. These include: Colonel Cathcart, Yossarian's commanding officer, whose consuming ambition to get his picture in the *Saturday Evening Post* motivates him to volunteer his command for every dangerous command, and to initiate prayers during briefing sessions ("I don't want any of this Kingdom of God or Valley of Death stuff. That's all too negative. . . . Couldn't we pray for a tighter bomb pattern?"), an idea he abandons only when he learns enlisted men pray to the same God; General Peckem, head of Special Services, whose strategic objective is to replace General Dreedle, the wing commander, capturing every bomber group in the U.S. Air Force ("If dropping bombs on the enemy isn't a special service, I wonder what in the world is"); Captain Black, the squadron intelligence officer, who inaugurates the Glorious Loyalty Oath Crusade in order to discomfort a rival, forcing all officers (except the rival, who is thereupon declared a Communist) to sign a new oath whenever they get their flak suits, their pay checks, or their haircuts; Lieutenant Scheisskopf, paragon of the parade ground, whose admiration for efficient formations makes him scheme to screw nickel-alloy swivels into every cadet's back for perfect ninety degree turns; and cadres of sadistic officers, club-happy MPs, and muddleheaded agents of the CID, two of whom, popping in and out of rooms like farcical private eyes, look for Washington Irving throughout the action, finally pinning the rap on the innocent chaplain.

These are Yossarian's antagonists, all of them reduced to a single exaggerated humor, and all identified by their totally mechanical attitude towards human life. Heller has a profound hatred for this kind of military mind, further anatomized in a wacky scene before the Action Board which displays his (and their) animosity in a manner both hilarious and scarifying. But Heller, at war with much larger forces than the army, has provided his book with much wider implications than a war novel. For the author (apparently sharing the Italian belief that vengeance is a dish which tastes best cold) has been nourishing his grudges for so long that they have expanded to include the post-war American world. Through the agency of grotesque comedy, Heller has found a way to confront the humbug, hypocrisy, cruelty, and sheer stupidity of our mass society—qualities which have made the few other Americans who care almost speechless with baffled rage—and through some miracle of prestidigitation, Pianosa has become a satirical microcosm for many of the macrocosmic idiocies of our time. Thus, the author flourishes his Juvenalian scourge at government-subsidized agriculture (and farmers, one of whom "spent every penny he didn't earn on new land to increase the amount of alfalfa he did not grow"); at the exploitation of American Indians, evicted from their oil-rich land; at smug psychiatrists; at bureaucrats and patriots; at acquisitive war widows; at high-spirited American boys; and especially, and most vindictively, at war profiteers.

This last satirical flourish, aimed at the whole mystique of corporation capitalism, is embodied in the fantastic adventures of Milo Minderbinder, the company mess officer, and a paradigm of good natured Jonsonian cupidity. Anxious to put the war on a business-like basis, Milo has formed a syndicate designed to corner the world market on all available foodstuffs, which he then sells to army messhalls at huge profits. Heady with success (his deals have made him Mayor of every town in Sicily, Vice-Shah of Oran, Caliph of Baghdad, Imam of Damascus, and the Sheik of Araby), Milo soon expands his activities, forming a private army which he hires out to the highest bidder. The climax of Milo's career comes when he fulfills a contract with the Germans to bomb and strafe his own outfit, directing his planes from the Pianosa control tower and justifying the action with the stirring war cry: "What's good for the syndicate is good for the country." Milo has almost succeeded in his ambition to pre-empt the field of war for private enterprise when he makes a fatal mistake: he has cornered the entire Egyptian cotton market and is unable to unload it anywhere. Having failed to pass it off to his own messhall in the form of chocolate-covered cotton, Milo is finally persuaded by Yossarian to bribe the American government to take it off his hands: "If you run into trouble, just tell everybody that the security of the country requires a strong domestic Egyptian cotton speculating industry." The Minderbinder sections—in showing the basic incompatibility of idealism and economics by satirizing the patriotic cant which usually accompanies American greed—illustrate the procedure of the entire book: the ruthless ridicule of hypocrisy through a technique of farce-fantasy, beneath which the demon of satire lurks, prodding fat behinds with a red-hot pitchfork.

It should be abundantly clear, then, that *Catch-22*, despite some of the most outrageous sequences since *A Night at the Opera*, is an intensely serious work. Heller has certain technical similarities to the Marx Brothers, Max Schulman, Kingsley Amis, Al Capp, and S. J. Perelman, but his mordant intelligence, closer to that of Nathanael West, penetrates the surface of the merely funny to expose a world of ruthless self-advancement, gruesome cruelty, and flagrant disregard for human life—a world, in short, very much like our own as seen through a magnifying glass, distorted for more perfect accuracy. Considering his indifference to surface reality, it is absurd to judge Heller by standards of psychological realism (or, for that matter, by conventional artistic standards at all, since his book is as formless as any picaresque epic). He is concerned entirely with that thin boundary of the surreal, the borderline between hilarity and horror, which, much like the apparent formlessness of the unconscious, has its own special integrity and coherence. Thus, Heller will never use comedy for its own sake; each joke has a wider significance in the intricate pattern, so that laughter becomes a prologue for some grotesque revelation. This gives the reader an effect of surrealistic dislocation, intensified by a weird, rather flat, impersonal style, full of complicated reversals, swift transitions, abrupt shifts in chronological time, and manipulated identities (e.g. if a private named Major Major Major is promoted to Major by a faulty IBM machine, or if a malingerer, sitting out a doomed mission, is declared dead through a bureaucratic error, then this remains their permanent fate), as if all mankind was determined by a mad and merciless mechanism.

Thus, Heller often manages to heighten the macabre obscenity of total war much more effectively through its gruesome comic aspects than if he had written realistic descriptions. And thus, the most delicate pressure is enough to send us over the line from farce into phantasmagoria. In the climactic chapter, in fact, the book leaves comedy altogether and becomes an eerie nightmare of terror. Here, Yossarian, walking through the streets of Rome as though through an Inferno, observes soldiers molesting drunken women, fathers beating ragged children, policemen clubbing innocent bystanders until the whole world seems swallowed up in the maw of evil:

> The night was filled with horrors, and he thought he knew how Christ must have felt as he walked through the world, like a psychiatrist through a ward of nuts, like a victim through a prison of thieves. . . . Mobs . . . mobs of policemen. . . . Mobs with clubs were in control everywhere.

Here, as the book leaves the war behind, it is finally apparent that Heller's comedy is his artistic response to his vision of transcendent evil, as if the escape route of laughter were the only recourse from a malignant world.

It is this world, which cannot be divided into boundaries or ideologies, that Yossarian has determined to resist. And so when his fear and disgust have reached the breaking point, he simply refuses to fly another mission. Asked by a superior what would happen if everybody felt the same way, Yossarian exercises his definitive logic and answers, "Then I'd be a damned fool to feel any other way." Having concluded a separate peace, Yossarian maintains it in the face of derision, ostracism, psychological pressure, and the threat of court martial. When he is finally permitted to go home if he will only agree to a shabby deal whitewashing Colonel Cathcart, however, he finds himself impaled on two impossible alternatives. But his unique logic, helped along by the precedent of an even more logical friend, makes him conclude that desertion is the better part of valor; and so (after an inspirational sequence which is the weakest thing in the book) he takes off for neutral Sweden—the only place left in the world, outside of England, where "mobs with clubs" are not in control.

Yossarian's expedient is not very flattering to our national ideals, being defeatist, selfish, cowardly, and unheroic. On the other hand, it is one of those sublime expressions of anarchic individualism without which all national ideals are pretty hollow anyway. Since the mass State, whether totalitarian or democratic, has grown increasingly hostile to Falstaffian irresponsibility, Yossarian's anti-heroism is, in fact, a kind of inverted heroism which we would do well to ponder. For, contrary to the armchair pronouncements of patriotic ideologues, Yossarian's obsessive concern for survival makes him not only *not* morally dead, but one of the most morally vibrant figures in recent literature—and a giant of the will beside those weary, wise and wistful prodigals in contemporary novels who always accommodate sadly to American life. I believe that Joseph Heller is one of the most extraordinary talents now among us. He has Mailer's combustible radicalism without his passion for violence and self-glorification; he has Bellow's gusto with his compulsion to affirm the unaffirmable; and he has Salinger's wit without his coquettish self-consciousness. Finding his absolutes in the freedom to *be,* in a world dominated by cruelty, carnage, inhumanity, and a rage to destroy itself, Heller has come upon a new morality based on an old ideal, the morality of refusal. Perhaps—now that Catch-22 has found its most deadly nuclear form—we have reached the point where even the logic of survival is unworkable. But at least we can still contemplate the influence of its liberating honesty on a free, rebellious spirit in this explosive, bitter, subversive, brilliant book.

T O M   W O L F E   ON

An American Dream
by Norman Mailer, 1965

In 1964, Norman Mailer took on the Dickensian-Dostoevskian challenge of writing An American Dream *in installments for* Esquire. *This risky "first" for an American novelist, coupled with the sensationalism of the book's plot, generated a storm of controversy to which satirist Tom Wolfe contributed this memorable essay entitled "Son of Crime and Punishment."*

Norman Mailer announced in the December 1963 issue of *Esquire,* in a column he had in there called "The Big Bite," that he was going to write a serialized novel under the old nineteenth-century pop magazine conditions, namely, in monthly installments, writing against a deadline every month. A lot of *pressure* and everything. Mailer worked the whole thing out with the editor of *Esquire,* Harold Hayes. The idea was to write the first chapter and then, after that went to press, he would write the second chapter; and after that one went to press, he would write the third one, and so on, through eight chapters, turning out one every thirty days, writing right up to the press time all the time.

The idea stirred up a lot of interest among literati and culturati in New York. For one thing—daring!—it was like *Dickens* or something. That comparison came up quite a bit—Dickens. It was going to be interesting to see if Mailer could voluntarily put himself inside the same kind of pressure cooker Dickens worked in and not merely endure but thrive on the pressure the way Dickens did. *Tour de force! Neo-Dickens! Courage under fire!* Actually, looking back on it, everybody should have figured out at the time that it really wasn't

Dickens that Mailer had in mind. Any old epopt of the Harvard EngLit like Norman Mailer would consider Dickens a lightweight. The hell with Charles Dickens. The writer Mailer had in mind was a heavyweight, Dostoevski. I will try to show in a moment, in the scholarly fashion, how specifically he had Dostoevski in mind.

The other thing that stirred up a lot of interest in this prospect of Mailer's was his personal history. Mailer had not written a novel in practically ten years when he started on this serial. Seventeen years ago, in 1948, Mailer had published a highly praised first novel, *The Naked and the Dead.* Among the military novels of the period, I would say it ranked second only to James Jones's *From Here to Eternity.* Mailer published his second novel, *Barbary Shore,* in 1951. The critics really bombed it. Somebody called it "a 1984 for D train winos." The D train on New York's IND subway line runs all the way from 205th Street in the Bronx to Coney Island and is great for sleeping it off. Mailer published his third novel, *The Deer Park,* in 1955. The critics bushwhacked him again. They cut him up, they *tenderized* him.

Mailer stopped publishing novels at that point, although he did try to write one, a kind of windy one, judging from excerpts. Yet during the next ten years, from then to now, Mailer became a bigger public figure writing no novels at all than he had by writing them. He was on television all the time and wrote articles here and there. He hung around with prizefighters the way Hemingway hung around with bullfighters, and he tried pot and existentialism and Negroes and did a great deal of brooding over God, freedom and immortality and the rest of it. He had a lot of good roughhousing ego and anger and showmanship and could always get an audience, even among people who didn't want to listen. *Happy Chutzpah!*

In 1960 his life really began to pick up momentum. He started to write articles for *Esquire,* reportage, which were by far his best work since *The Naked and the Dead.* The first big one was on John Kennedy's nomination. Mailer, like Gore Vidal and James Michener, had gotten very much wrapped up in politics and gotten a mystic crush on Kennedy, much the way the stock liberals of another generation had fallen for the first American "left aristocrat," Franklin Roosevelt. Mailer announced on TV that he was going to run for mayor of New York.

He also committed a number of acts that firmly established him in the Wild Boy of Western Literature tradition. Holy Beasts! That wasn't why he committed them, but that was the upshot of it. First off, in June 1960, he was arrested in the boho resort of Province-town, on Cape Cod, for getting drunk and hailing a police car with the cry "Taxi! Taxi!" because it had a light on top of it. His head was cracked open in a fracas at the station house, but he got some revenge on the police by acting as his own lawyer at the trial and giving the police a going-over on the stand. On November 14, 1960, he was arrested about 4 A.M. in Birdland, the Broadway jazz club, after an argument over a check. Six days later he stabbed his second wife, Adele, after a party in their apartment on Ninety-fourth Street. She refused to press charges, and he got off with a suspended sentence, but the case got a lot of mileage in the papers.

He was all over the papers again in 1961 when they pulled the curtain on him during a poetry reading at the Young Men's Hebrew Association because his poems were getting too gamey for even that liberal atmosphere. In 1962, more headlines—Mailer married Lady Jeanne Campbell, daughter of the Duke of Argyll and granddaughter of Lord Beaverbrook. Their courtship, their marriage, their breakup, their divorce in 1963, the old Juarez route—people were fascinated by all this and talked about it all the time. The pace kept picking up and picking up, even to the point where Mailer hired a hall, Carnegie Hall, in 1963 and got up on a podium and orated, read from his own works, preached, shouted, held colloquies with the audience, great stuff. He also started writing his *Esquire* column, "The Big Bite," which kind of flamed out—but then—brave bull!—he began his serial novel, *An American Dream*, in *Esquire*'s January 1964 issue.

The story, as it unfolded, ran like this: Stephen Rojack, war hero, ex-congressman, author, professor, television star, and accomplished stud, is separated from his wife, Deborah, a forceful woman who has noble blood in her veins and an English accent. He loves her but he hates her, because she is all the time humiliating him. He visits her apartment one night, they exchange their usual venomous *mots,* he gets mad and strangles her to death. He throws her body out the window onto the East River Drive, where it causes a five-car pile-up. Brought to a halt by the whole mess is a car bearing Eddie Ganucci, the Mafia boss, and Cherry, nightclub singer and Mafia love slave. Rojack and Cherry fall in love more or less at first sight. Rojack claims his wife committed suicide right in front of his eyes. The bulk of the story concerns whether or not the police can pin the murder on Rojack and, more important, whether or not he is strong enough to withstand the various pressures the whole thing puts on him. The police put him through an ingenious interrogation, but he maintains his cool and is released for the time being. He turns to Cherry, takes up with her, and beats up her Negro ex-lover, one of America's great popular singers, Shago Martin. Rojack is now ready to face up to his dead wife's father, fabulously wealthy, powerful Barney Oswald Kelly. They have a talk-out in Kelly's Waldorf Towers apartment and a climactic ordeal-by-courage.

The scramble to meet the deadlines in writing the serial was just as wild as Mailer himself had predicted it would be. Hayes, *Esquire*'s editor, kept the layout forms open for Mailer's installments practically up to the morning of the day the presses had to run. A lot of roaring around, one understands, gasps, groans, desperation, but even in all that Mailer wasn't really doing things the Charles Dickens way. Dickens was rather cool about the whole process. Sometimes Dickens used to come down in the living room and write down there with four or five guests sitting around and talking with his wife. He would put his head up from time to time and interject a remark when something in the conversation caught his ear. That cool, hip Dickens. But Mailer wasn't even thinking about Dickens. He was going to take on Dostoevski.

Mailer has always been measuring himself against other writers. He has been saying, Is Jones, Willingham, Capote or Kerouac or whoever as good as me, long after most literati regarded Mailer as no longer even in the competition. In one essay, "The Other Talent in the Room," he managed to tell off most of the prominent novelists in the country as inferior men—weaklings mostly, no guts, no cool, can't drink, you know?—as well as artists. Well, here he had demolished all his contemporaries, and so now he had nothing but a few dead but durable giants to look to. Hemingway, with whom Mailer identifies quite a bit, had the same streak. Hemingway once announced that he had beaten Turgenev's brains out and there was only one champ left to take on, Tolstoi. Mailer has even stronger motives, personal ones, to look to Dostoevski.

Dostoevski, like Mailer, had a solid decade in his young manhood when he didn't write a thing. In 1849 Dostoevski was convicted as a revolutionary and sent to Siberia. He didn't return to St. Petersburg and start writing until 1859, at the age of thirty-eight. Mailer had a hiatus almost that long, 1954 to 1964. Nobody sent Mailer off anywhere, but the result was the same. There he was, forty-one years old, and hadn't written a novel since he was thirty-one. Anyway, Mailer knew something about Dostoevski's comeback that isn't popularly known, namely, that Dostoevski did it all, suddenly burst forth as the greatest writer in Russia, by writing serialized novels under monthly deadline pressure. Dostoevski's greatest works, *Crime and Punishment, The Gambler, The Idiot, The Possessed, The Brothers Karamozov,* first appeared in magazines, most of them in *Russky Vestnik.*

Dostoevski wrote Katkov, the editor of *Russky Vestnik,* offering him the first in this incredible streak of magazine fiction, *Crime and Punishment,* one September (1865), the same month of the year Mailer picked to offer *An American Dream* to Hayes at *Esquire.* I haven't talked to Mailer about this, but I wouldn't be surprised if he didn't decide to follow Dostoevski's example just that closely. He has a great vein of nineteenth-century superstition in him, a lot of voodoo about *cancer,* for example, the personal outlook of the kidney cells, incredible gothic theorizing. Mailer apparently has read Dostoevski's letters and diaries. In his prospectus for the serial project in the December 1963 *Esquire,* he cites a passage from

Dostoevski's journals telling how he used to work all night long, in the lucid moments between attacks of epilepsy, in order to keep going and meet the deadlines.

Dostoevski's performance in 1866, the year *Crime and Punishment* started appearing in *Russky Vestnik,* was prodigious. The first installment appeared in January—the month of the year Mailer's serial began—and there were eight installments in all—the same as with Mailer. In the same year (1866) Dostoevski also signed a contract to do a novel for another magazine by November 1. If he didn't make the deadline, he would suffer a heavy financial penalty, and the publisher, Stellovsky, would get the right to publish all of Dostoevski's novels, in book form, past and future, without giving him anything. As of October 1 Dostoevski still had about one-fourth of *Crime and Punishment* to write and hadn't written a line of the novel for Stelovski. On October 4 he hired a stenographer—later he married her—and started dictating *The Gambler* right out of his head. He finished it on October 30, a forty-thousand-word novel that is considered his most perfect novel from a technical point of view. The next day he sat down and started dictating the last two installments of *Crime and Punishment* and was home safe on both novels.

All of this must have had a double appeal for Mailer. First of all, here was a man who made his comeback in a big way through the magazine serial. Second, he did it through a *roman à thèse,* a philosophical novel. Mailer has a terrible hang-up on the *roman à thèse.* The reason for the failure of both *Barbary Shore* and *The Deer Park* was chiefly their soggy tractlike nature. But *Crime and Punishment* was a *roman à thèse* that did make it, and *An American Dream*—well, there are a great many things in Mailer's book that resemble *Crime and Punishment* in plot, structure, theme and detail.

Mailer's book, like *Crime and Punishment,* concerns a sensitive young man who murders a woman, and the story in each case hinges on whether or not the hero is going to have the existential—to use a term Mailer likes—the existential willpower, the courage, to weather the storm that follows. In each case, the hero turns to a quasi-prostitute for emotional sustenance immediately after the crime—Raskolnikov turns to Sonia in *Crime and Punishment* and Rojack turns to Cherry in Mailer's book. In both cases the hero comes together with the girl as the result of a wreck in the street. In both cases the hero confesses his guilt to the girl as a pledge of faith. In both books he undergoes a long, intriguing interrogation by the authorities, in which the questioner seems to know he did it and is trying to trap him emotionally and verbally into confessing. In both cases it is technically, circumstantially, within the power of the hero to get out of the whole thing without admitting his guilt. Most curiously of all, Mailer, like Dostoevski, has chosen to add to the story a short, final chapter, called "Epilogue"—rather weak and pointless in each case—in which the hero goes off into some kind of wasteland. Raskolnikov is sent off to Siberia, even though the book has a very powerful and dramatic natural ending with the confession itself. Mailer has Rojack drive off into the Nevada desert.

Dostoevski is not a great deal more profound than Mailer, but Dostoevski always had the good fortune of never being able to make his ideas dominate his characters. Dostoevski is always starting out to have some characters express one of his ideas and very quickly the whole thing gets out of hand, Dostoevski gets wrapped up in the character rather than the idea, as in Marmeladov's saloon scene. Dostoevski resembled Dickens in this respect. Both seemed to have such powers of imagination that characters grew in concept during the very process of the writing, with all sorts of baroque and humorous curlicues of the psyche coming out. Mailer's trouble is that whenever he has a theory, which is pretty often, he always kills some poor son of a bitch in his book with it. In *An American Dream* he crushes his hero, Rojack, with too much thinking in the first fourteen and a half pages and kills him off for the rest of the novel.

At the outset we get a picture of this brave, talented, and highly placed man—hero, author, scholar, TV star, socialite, sex maestro—who for some reason is in a hopeless funk, foundering, sinking down through a lot of rancid gothic metaphysics. One is reminded of a remark Turgenev made about Dostoevski's weakest novel, *Raw Youth*: "I took a glance into that chaos. God! What sour stuff—the stench of the sickroom, unprofitable gibberish, psychological excavation." By page 13 Rojack is out on somebody's apartment terrace thinking about jumping, and by then he is already so boring and logorrheic, one's impulse is to put the book down and say, Jump. Mailer was clearly trying to establish a Dostoevskian mood of the Troubled Genius in this passage. What he does mainly, however, is give one the feeling that here is some old gasbag who doesn't know when he is well off. Rojack, like all of Mailer's people, doesn't know how to laugh. He opens his mouth and—aaaagh— just brays in a kind of sterile Pentecostal frenzy. Mailer could still have salvaged Rojack, I suspect, if he had only written the novel in the third person instead of the first. Use of the first person leads Mailer to have his hero think himself into all sorts of puling funk holes all the time.

If I were editing *An American Dream*, I would cut out the first fourteen pages and about half of page 15, through the sentence that ends ". . . they were flinching as the wind rode by." That sentence is too nineteenth-century gothic anyway, all this business of the wind riding by. The wind doesn't do much riding in this era of meteorology, it just blows. I would start the book with the next sentence, "A familiar misery was on me." That's a little Poe-like, but it's all right. If the book starts right there, no background information needs to be added. The whole thing starts off fast from that point and we have a good little action story going. One big advantage is that now, in the scene where Rojack starts having words with his wife, which is a fine scene, actually, we can have some kind of sympathy for him, because his wife is obviously such an accomplished bitch. We can even sympathize with his choking her to death and we can pull for the poor guy to outwit the police. As the book is actually written, however, one's first impulse is to hope that Rojack *gets his*, too.

The next passage that has to go is pages 41 through 46, which describes perhaps the most ludicrous love scene in fiction. Rojack starts *thinking* again, that is the trouble. He gets this *theory* that after he murders his wife he has got to make love to her maid, Ruta, by alternating, rapidly, from conventional copulation to buggery, back and forth. He does so, and he is *thinking* all the time.

It is all wrapped up with God, the Devil, and the Proper Orgasm, and even aside from certain quaint anatomical impossibilities, it is all told in some kind of great gothic Lake Country language of elegance. It sounds, actually, with all these gods, devils, and orgasms running around, like some Methodist minister who has discovered orgone theory and, with a supreme ecumenical thrust, has decided to embrace both John Wesley and Wilhelm Reich.

If we get rid of that scene, we are quickly back into a stretch of fine fast-paced action, almost like James M. Cain. The spell breaks in the last chapter, however, when Rojack starts thinking his head off again during the confrontation with Barney Oswald Kelly. The scene bogs down further in another difficulty of the book, unreal dialogue. Kelly has a lengthy speech in this chapter and keeps slipping into such rhetoric as, "I thought myself a competitive fellow, just consider—I had to be nearly as supersensational with sex as with *dinero*, and Bess and I gave each other some glorious good times in a row; up would climb the male ego; applause from Bess was accolade from Cleopatra; then swish! she'd vanish."

Aside from the coy expressions, such as *dinero*, all this doesn't . . . *parse*. One reason, perhaps, is that Mailer brings his big characters on one by one in this book like cameo parts in a play like *The Days and Nights of Beebee Fenstermaker*. They have just one big scene each, and so they have to start talking like maniacs right from the word go and ricochet around all over the place and tell their whole life stories while Rojack, who is *thinking* all the time, lards up the scene a little more.

Even so, once the first fourteen and a half pages of the book are out of the way, Mailer exhibits much of the best things he has going for him, his drive, his pace, his gift of narrative, his nervous excitement, things Cain and Raymond Chandler had, but not too many other American novelists. Using the serial form—ending each chapter cliff-hanger style—Mailer creates excellent suspense—in fact, in much of the book Mailer moves, probably unconsciously, in the direction of Cain and shows great promise. In the context of a Cain adventure, Mailer's gothic attitude toward sex—which Cain shares—a great deal of new-sentimental business about how making love to a broad is all mixed up with death and fate and how you can tell your fortune by the quality of the orgasm—all this is not embarrassing in the context of a Cain novel like *The Postman Always Rings Twice*.

Of course, Mailer cannot match Cain in writing dialogue, creating characters, setting up scenes or carrying characters through a long story. But he is keener than Cain in summoning up smells, especially effluvia. I think Norman Mailer can climb into the same ring as James M. Cain. He's got to learn some fundamentals, such as how to come out of his corner faster. But that can be picked up. A good solid Cain-style opening goes like this:

"They threw me off the hay truck about noon . . ."

WILFRID SHEED ON

Slaughterhouse-Five
by Kurt Vonnegut, Jr., 1969

Dismissed as a science-fiction writer by the critics for the first decade of his literary career, Kurt Vonnegut suddenly found himself at the center of a cult of youthful admirers in the late sixties. When Slaughterhouse-Five appeared in 1969, there were 1.5 million Americans in Vietnam, and Vonnegut's "fiction of witness," as Wilfrid Sheed called it in this review from Life, had a particular resonance for the times.

Kurt Vonnegut was present as a prisoner of war (so it goes, as he would say) at the Dresden fire-bomb raid in 1945—possibly the greatest atrocity ever committed by Americans and certainly the quietest. Most of the public hadn't heard of it until well after the Nuremberg trials. Vonnegut says it took him more than twenty years to write a novel about it, and in a sense he hasn't written one yet. As though blinded by the glare of the fire bombs, he has turned his back on the raid and written a parable instead.

His hero is called Billy Pilgrim—who represents the kind of pilgrim we are down to by this century—on his way from Dresden to whatever heaven you can still believe in after Dresden. Billy is World War II's Sad Sack, with all the comedy drained out of him. (A funny Sad Sack takes the curse off war and Vonnegut wants the curse left on and doubled.) Billy is not even the universal victim, who testifies to the human spirit, because his spirit is long since broken. He is a vegetable, he is below the human requirements for pity or laughter. He is not even a "character" anymore; a pilgrim of the period was moved along by someone else's boot, so did not need to be.

We first stumble over Billy wandering vaguely behind enemy

lines, numb with pain, a heel missing from one of his shoes, finding "no important differences between walking and standing still." Vonnegut is an expert comic writer, and a word from him would have us howling like children at Pilgrim's predicament. But the author fixes us with a liverish eye and the word never comes.

To his apathetic relief, Billy is captured, then kicked around like a rag doll, stuffed into a tiny overcoat and stashed away in a pig shelter called Slaughterhouse-Five—all the makings of a Christ-figure except that he is a vegetable and doesn't qualify. His colleagues watch him like rats, beyond compassion or instruction, kept alive and warm by dull animal hate. His captors despise him. It takes all the fun out of war to find you have been fighting such wrecks as this. Vonnegut will have no Christs giving value to Dresden, any more than he will permit clowns.

As Billy bobs along like garbage in a sewer, beyond ridicule and pride, wishing only for a place in the dark to move his bowels, the city is hit. The incident is almost casual. At this level of Goyaesque human depravity, what did you expect? A strategically meaningless obliteration of an open city seems the most natural thing in the world. Up to now the reader may have been consoling himself that Vonnegut has been overstating the moral squalor of war. But suddenly you see that decisions like Dresden and Hiroshima can only be discussed in a context of moral squalor. A fable worthy of Dresden requires characters out of a bestiary. The enlisted men must be brought down to the level of the Brass and the Brass down to the level of the Atrocity. And if you say, but they're subhuman, you've got the point about Dresden precisely.

How does the human soul recover from having been a rat or a vegetable, an aggressor or a victim? The rats have it easy. They join rat races, become respectable citizens or old soldiers who write histories of gallantry. But victims have more accurate memories, and Billy, years after Dresden, still carries the war on his nerve-ends like radiation burns.

But peace is hard on the vegetables, because their minds froze during the nightmare, and they are forced to remember it without anesthetic exactly as it was. Pilgrim is doomed to play his humiliation over and over in his mind; and it is so glued to his nerve-ends that to remember is to re-experience totally. His vegetable passivity recorded all the things that the rats missed, or forgot, or lied about later. And civilian life will never be more to him than a shadow, or cheap imitation, of war after that.

Pilgrim's solution is to invent a heaven, out of twentieth-century materials, where Good Technology triumphs over Bad Technology. His scripture is Science Fiction, man's last good fantasy. He imagines that he is whisked off to a planet called Tralfamadore, where suffering and death are trivial. "When a Tralfamadorian sees a corpse, all he thinks is that the dead person is in bad condition in that particular moment," but there are plenty of other moments. The past is as real as the present, and you just pick the tense of your choice.

This does not cure Billy of the war. But now, when his mind returns to it, he can take his Tralfamadorian wisdom with him to cushion the pain. And he can even make believe he had the wisdom all along. He now imagines that as he was walking his Calvary, he already had visions of heaven to sustain him—a benign lie of his own about war.

This gets Vonnegut into some delicate time-switch writing, which would have many writers wheezing—a character remembering a past in which he foresees the future—but he does it with splendid art and simplicity. *Slaughterhouse-Five* is written with nerve-racking control: a funny book at which you are not permitted to laugh, a sad book without tears, a book of carefully strangled emotions. A tale told in a slaughterhouse.

Vonnegut may get a lot of mail saying that it wasn't like that, that there were many acts of nobility among the seediest war prisoners and possibly even that the people who decided to bomb Dresden were deeply troubled men. He does admit, in a curiously mannered introduction, that he is not going to give the war-lovers a chance: "There won't be a part for John Wayne."

But beyond that he says only, like Pilgrim, "I was there." It is a fiction of witness. This is what it felt like to be on the ground that day. This is what the human face looked like by firelight, specifically the American face. Billy's ratlike companions are not so much people as moral equivalents. Vonnegut does not theorize outside of his parable. The Tralfamadorians (who sound like American technocrats after a course in Zen) expect more wars and so does he. He just wants you to know how it was in Dresden.

So—war drives people crazy, or at least, craziness may be the most honorable response to it. It has its compensations. Pilgrim, the all-American escapist, demonstrating human love techniques to the Tralfamadorians, with the aid of one Montana Wildhack of Hollywood, winds up the happiest man in the book.

ACKNOWLEDGMENTS

We are grateful to the authors, publishers, literary agents and executors who granted permission to use copyrighted material in this work. These and other sources listed below were used to compile this work.

Henry James's "Hawthorne, *The Scarlet Letter*," from Chapter V of *Hawthorne* by Henry James (1879).

Introduction to *Moby-Dick*. Copyright © 1984, 1956 by Alfred Kazin. Reprinted by permission of the author.

"Making de White Boss Frown" by Anthony Burgess. Copyright © 1966 by Encounter Ltd., Vol. xxvii, No. 1.

T. S. Eliot's Introduction to *Huckleberry Finn* by Mark Twain. Reprinted by permission of Faber & Faber, Ltd.

Lionel Trilling on *The Bostonians*. From *The Opposing Self*, copyright © 1955 by Lionel Trilling; renewed 1983 by Diana Trilling and James Trilling. Reprinted by permission of Harcourt Brace Jovanovich, Inc.

Introduction to *The Red Badge of Courage* by Stephen Crane. Copyright © 1960 by V. S. Pritchett. Reprinted from World's Classics edition of *The Red Badge of Courage and Other Stories* by Stephen Crane (1960; reissued in paperback 1969) by permission of Oxford University Press.

Introduction by Irving Howe. From *The House of Mirth* by Edith Wharton, edited by Irving Howe. Introduction copyright © 1962 by Holt, Rinehart & Winston, Inc. Reprinted by permission of Henry Holt and Company, Inc.

"Babbitt," by Rebecca West, from *The New Statesman*, October 21, 1922. Copyright 1922 by Rebecca West.

H. L. Mencken's Introduction to *An American Tragedy* by Theodore Dreiser. Reprinted by permission of the Enoch Pratt Free Library in accordance with the terms of the will of H. L. Mencken.

"The Romance of Money" by Malcolm Cowley, from *Three Novels by F. Scott Fitzgerald*, Charles Scribner's Sons, 1953. Copyright renewal © 1961 by Malcolm Cowley. Reprinted by permission of the author.

Ford Madox Ford's Introduction to *A Farewell to Arms*. Copyright 1932 by Random House, Inc. Reprinted from *A Farewell to Arms* by Ernest Hemingway, by permission of Random House, Inc.

Acknowledgments

Maxwell Perkins on Thomas Wolfe's *Look Homeward, Angel*. Reprinted from the *Harvard Library Bulletin;* Vol. 1, No. 3 (Autumn 1947). Copyright 1947 by the President and Fellows of Harvard College.

Introduction by William Faulkner. Copyright © 1932, renewed 1959 by William Faulkner. Reprinted from *Sanctuary* by William Faulkner, by permission of Random House, Inc.

"John Dos Passos and *1919*" from *Literary and Philosophical Essays by Jean-Paul Sartre*, translated by Annette Michelson. Copyright © 1955 by Rider & Company. Taken from "A propos John Dos Passos and *1919*." Extracts from *Situations 1* by Jean Paul Sartre © Editions Gallimard 1948.

Introduction by Budd Schulberg. Time Reading Program—*The Day of the Locust*. Introduction by Bud Schulberg. Copyright © 1965 by Time-Life Books.

"On Rereading *Native Son*" by David Bradley. Originally published in *The New York Times Magazine*. Reprinted by permission of The Wendy Weill Agency, Inc. Copyright © 1986 by David Bradley.

Introduction by Tennessee Williams. "Carson McCullers, *Reflections in a Golden Eye*." Copyright 1949 by Tennessee Williams. Reprinted by permission of New Directions Publishing Corporation.

"Man Underground" by Saul Bellow. Reprinted by permission of Harriet Wasserman Literary Agency, Inc., as agent for the author. Copyright © 1952, 1980 by Saul Bellow.

"The Logic of Survival in a Lunatic World" by Robert Brustein. Reprinted by permission of *The New Republic*; copyright © 1961 by The New Republic, Inc.

"Son of *Crime and Punishment*" by Tom Wolfe originally appeared in *Book Week* (March 14, 1965). Copyright © 1965 by The Washington Post Company. Reprinted by permission of the author.

"Requiem to Billy Pilgrim's Progress" by Wilfrid Sheed. Copyright © 1969, 1972 by Wilfrid Sheed. Reprinted by permission of the author.